Ferriday, Louisiana

Ferriday, Louisiana

ELAINE DUNDY

DONALD I. FINE, INC.
NEW YORK

Library of Congress Cataloging-in-Publication Data

Dundy, Elaine.
Ferriday, Louisiana / by Elaine Dundy.
p.   cm.
ISBN 1-55611-144-4
1. Ferriday (La.)   I. Title.
F379.F47D86   1990
976.3'73—dc20   89-45341
CIP

Manufactured in the United States of America

10 9 8 7 6 5 4 3 2 1

Designed by Folio Graphics Company, Inc.

ACKNOWLEDGMENTS

I would like to take this opportunity to thank Sandy Brokaw for his information, his help and his encouragement, but most of all for our very first conversation, out of which the idea of this book came into being. I would also like to thank Jason Pomerance whose perfect pitch made him so invaluable to me as assistant and consultant. My thanks also to Dr. Ronald A. Gershman for his good counsel. Peter Guralnick's excellent books on American music, with their detailed portraits of performers in their historical backgrounds, were of immense help to me. I am forever indebted to Professor David Evans for so generously allowing me extensive use of his articles, as well as the content of our correspondence and conversations, particularly on the subject of Peewee Whittaker. My chapter on Peewee pays close attention to his article on Hezekiah and the Houserockers written for *Louisiana Folk Life*, Volume 7, Number 2 (October 1982), from which excerpts of Peewee's and Hezekiah's quotes have been reproduced (see bibliography). David Evans, one of the most active and creative forces in advancing the awareness and appreciation of North and South American ethnic music, is Professor of Music at Memphis State University and Director of Graduate Degree Programs in Ethnomusicology. He is also a distinguished field worker in the area of black southern historical blues music and musicians and the producer and recording engineer for Memphis State's Highwater Recording Company featuring ethnic musicians. I would also like to thank Howard K. Smith for the stimulating and informative interview he gave me. This is the second book in which it is my pleasure to thank my colleague Roy Turner who aided and accompanied me in two of my visits to Ferriday. From the very beginning of this project, his comments on the manuscript were incisive and insightful.

Of the many citizens of Ferriday who gave so liberally of their time, allowing me to spend many hours with them, interviewing them in depth and who made my visits to Ferriday such welcome adventures, I would like to thank: Blanche Chauvin, Helen Warden, Mae Jones, Guy Serio, Mrs. Ben Green, Peewee Whittaker, Doris Morris, Reverend Son Swaggart, Nadine Comer, George Comer, Austin Wilson, R. T. Bonnette, Clyde Webber, Sam Hanna, Kathleen Stevens, Diane Brackenridge, Sammy Davis, Jr., (of Ferriday) Joe Pasternack, Jr., Hubert Lee McGlothin, Glen McGlothin, Joe-Jim Lee, Richard Alwood, Caroline Lewis, Judge Glen Gremillion, Jeffrey Gremillion, Dan Richey, Deborah Elaine, Burt Taunton, Rhett Powell, Paul Houghton, Russell Campbell, Tommy Latham, George Latham, Ira Rogillio, Frances Thomas Smith, Kathleen Winston, Woody Davis, Trish Gillespie, Gloria Brocato, Claudia Cooper, Joan Pitcher, Ocee Evans, Jane Huff, Gay Bradford, Reverend Huey Bradford, and the children Brandy Brixey and Nanci Newton.

I would like to single out for very special thanks Mrs. U. B. "Jo" Evans, Betty Ferrell, Edna Gilley Mequet, Marty Nathanson, Hiram "Pete" Gregory, Mickey Gilley, and Frankie Terrell. It is impossible to convey the sheer pleasure I felt as each Ferridian led me to more and more discoveries.

I am indebted also to Marguerite Littman and Wilton Wynn for their insights pertaining to growing up in northeast Louisiana.

Lastly, I am grateful to my fine editor, Lisa Healy.

CONTENTS

Ferriday, Louisiana

1

MISSION FERRIDAY

"So the Lord spoke to Leona Sumrall and told her that He wanted her to come to Ferriday. She said God spoke to her and said these words. 'I have some jewels in Ferriday, valuable treasures,' He said, 'unnoticed by the world but,' said God, 'if you will have patience they will come forth.' "

I am hearing these astonishing words from Jimmy Swaggart's father, Reverend Son Swaggart, aged seventy-three and himself still a preacher, as we sit talking in his trailer home on 8th Street in Ferriday.

He is telling me how it all began—that remarkable happening that took place over fifty years ago which would convert him, his family and his relatives to Christianity. He talks of how in the summer of 1936 Leona Sumrall, a seventeen-year-old girl on her knees praying for guidance, was answered by God with the aforementioned prophecy; how she, obeying that voice, set forth directly with her mother on the road that was to culminate in the founding of the Assembly of God Church in Ferriday. And so it seems that the church which was to be the cradle of the infant

1

cousins Jimmy Swaggart, Jerry Lee Lewis and Mickey Gilley, the cradle that would be rocked so energetically by their respective young mothers, was founded on a vision.

And so it also seems that in order to accomplish the feat of saving this turbulent, quarrelsome clan of farmers, uprooted in the Depression and reduced to picking cotton on other people's farms, from chaos, drunkenness and despair, someone had to be inspired by an act of faith beyond human comprehension.

And as for Leona Sumrall herself, not only in literature but in life, there are as many examples of teenage virgins visited by religious visions as there are of them visited by poltergeists.

Accounts recently written by both Leona and her brother Lester Sumrall fill in the whole picture.

The youngest of seven children, Leona was born of a poor family in New Orleans. Subsequently, the family lived in Mississippi, Alabama and Florida. Somewhere along the way her mother was saved and received the baptism of the Holy Spirit in one of the Holiness churches.* She began holding prayer meetings in people's homes and saw to it that her children regularly attended Sunday school in these churches. In the background of their childhood loomed 225 pounds worth of irate Irish father who hated preachers and excoriated them as beggars. But he soon faded away as they got on with life.

The brother closest to Leona in age and ties of affection was Lester Sumrall, now a world renowed evangelist with global missions. After a riotous, rebellious adolescence, followed by a miraculous recovery from TB, he became a traveling preacher. His sister Leona, as young as fourteen, would accompany him to meetings, playing her guitar and singing. The particular sect of the Holiness church they joined was the Assemblies of God. In 1936, when Lester

*"Pentecostal" and "Holiness" are used interchangeably to include all the charismatic sects. In fact, the specific Pentecostal church has doctrinal differences from the Assemblies of God. Its members use "Assemblies" to denote the church in general and "Assembly" to denote a specific one. The same shall be done here.

embarked on his first mission to Australia, Leona returned to her mother in Mobile, Alabama. Though deeply missing her brother, Leona was nevertheless keen to try her own wings. Earnestly both mother and daughter prayed for God's guidance. The answer came in the form of an invitation from an uncle to stay with him in a little town in Louisiana called Waterproof (which had to be moved three times before it could properly live up to its name) on the Mississippi River.

Arriving in Waterproof, Mother and Leona immediately began holding prayer meetings, and it was during this time that Leona may be said to have found herself with the exhilarating discovery that she loved to preach. She never looked back.

Word of Leona's gift spread, and before long the two women received an offer to pastor a church in the town of St. Joseph farther up the river. Curiously, something seemed to keep holding them back. Leona's God, it seems, was not only ready to indicate what she should do, but what she shouldn't. She prayed. It was then that God told her to go to Ferriday, some sixteen miles south of Waterproof. Mother, who is never called by any other appellation, presumably was getting the same guidance, but she needed Leona's confirmation. This sets the tone of their future relationship: the first and last word—and most of them in between—would always be Leona's.

The more they learned about Ferriday—that it was a wicked town, that it was a regular event there for someone to be stabbed or shot, that it was dangerous to drive through after dark—the more certain Leona was that God was leading them there to uncover His jewels and treasures. The uncle, confronted with their determination, merely asked them when they wanted to go. In less than an hour, they were on their way, brave women to reject a firm offer in favor of the unknown. It should be noted here that the Assemblies of God was well ahead of the most liberal religious denominations of the day in accepting women as preachers.

It is clear that once in Ferriday, Leona may have had her head in heaven, but her feet were firmly planted on the ground as she went about setting up her territory in an inspiringly businesslike way. Starting at the top, she called first on the town's mayor, Mr. Vogt, owner of its only drugstore. Leona marched into his office "so full of enthusiasm I could hardly contain myself" and asked him to grant them a permit to hold a youth revival in the town. "I will attract the youth!" she rhapsodized, "God wants to change this town!" The mayor, perhaps feeling that youth could stand reviving in this wicked town, gave the Sumralls the permit and a substantial check as well. From there they proceeded to find a vacant lot on which to hold their meetings. The owner of the lot turned out to be a Mr. Corbett, one of the richest men in town. Face to face with him, Leona reiterated her message. Corbett also succumbed, and Leona, with admirable foresight, got his signature on a paper which gave her the desired lot for an indefinite period of time. Now came the legwork, literally, for the two women had no car and traipsed from door to door stirring up people with their enthusiasm. A reluctant church organization yielded up a secondhand piano, a pianist and some Bible students. A sawmill gave them lumber for plank seats and a platform. Workers were talked into putting it together. A small apartment and groceries were found to accommodate them. Every evening Leona's feet were bloody from their long day's exertions.

The success of the teenage stranger as she struck at the town's power bases, bending them to her will, must be visualized to be appreciated. A pretty, even an appealing female stranger, so aggressively alight, so bursting with demands, might have been met with polite deflection had it not been for one factor in her favor. Though Leona alone did the talking and convincing, she was chaperoned every step of the way by a smiling, comfortable-looking mother whose bearing and behavior made clear to all her role as follower, not leader. What more might Joan of Arc have accomplished had she taken along her mother?

Added to all this was the stir they created walking down the streets dressed entirely in white. "I'll never forget those two ladies," says Mickey Gilley's sister Edna, known as the Popcorn Girl because she dispensed popcorn and candy at

Leona and Mother Sumrall, founders of the Assembly of God
Church in Ferriday, 1936. *(Credit: Edna Gilley Mequet private collection.)*

the Arcade Theatre. "I was twelve years old at the time, and
I would see them coming down the street looking like two
angels. Leona had beautiful black wavy hair that she wore
loose, but what made them look like angels was that they
always wore white dresses that came down to their ankles
and had flowing sleeves, and I never remember seeing them
in anything but that." Was this touch of the theatrical for a
studied effect? Of course it was. The point need not be
labored; in many other churches, the concerns of preachers
may also be labeled theatrical whether in splendid rituals or
dynamic preaching.

At the very first open air meeting in Ferriday, Leona
opened her Bible to Revelation 21:8 and read aloud: *"But the
fearful, and unbelieving, and the abominable, and murderers,
and whoremongers, and sorcerers, and idolators, and all liars,
shall have their part in the lake which burneth with fire and
brimstone: which is the second death."*

The audience, instead of receiving this news suitably
alarmed, subdued or at least reflective, burst into laughter.
After the meeting they explained to her that in Ferriday,

they were *all* fearful, unbelieving, abominable, and some were murderers. And so it went; every night at the meetings, she was dealing with drunkards, gamblers, prostitutes, bootleggers, liars and thieves. As she put it, "Every sin one could imagine seemed represented . . . I never knew until I went to Ferriday that the devil could be so mean to people."

The devil could be pretty mean to Leona, too. In the first week, a mob of ruffians accosted a member of the congregation threatening to "run those two women out of town if they don't leave tonight." They were told, "The youngest lady is in charge. She is as strong as iron." The mob followed Leona home. Calmly, she turned and bade them a firm goodnight. Shamefaced, they backed off.

The open air revivals went on all summer. Law-abiding men and women wanting to lead good, moral lives became attracted to her message. The rains came and still the people attended the meetings, an umbrella in one hand, a Bible in the other. The weather turned cold. A tent was erected. Then the Sumralls decided that the time had come to build an Assembly of God Church in Ferriday.

There was by now a nucleus of people they could count on, not only the rich and powerful, but the poor and powerless: specifically, those who lived on Mississippi Avenue, which was known as the Mason-Dixon line because it was the dividing line between the black and white communities. Among the most fervent was a family of barbers, the McGlothins, who would produce eleven children. The mother, Lillian, who was to become "one of the saints of the church," had been praying for just such a church long before the Sumralls arrived: a church unlike the others in Ferriday, a church of their own, especially for poor people like them, with a God they could love and understand, who would listen to their pleas and help them bear their burdens—in short, a God who would be on their side. Lillian and many others like her would embrace the kind of church where they were encouraged to release their pent-up feelings, where they could become active, exuberant participants throughout the service, praising the Lord out loud, shedding tears, jumping up, dancing, speaking in tongues when moved, instead of a church in which participation was limited to an Amen now and then and a couple of hymns.

The Assemblies of God is a charismatic sect which insists on the reality of the supernatural, particularly of the Holy Spirit, on which they place their main emphasis. It is a church which believes its worshipers can be saved, born again and anointed by the Holy Spirit whose seven gifts are: counsel, fear of the Lord, fortitude, piety, understanding, wisdom and knowledge, some of which gifts surely no one on this planet would be loath to receive.

What is not generally known is that, not just in the South but in the Midwest and West, the Assemblies of God, from its inception in 1914, became the fastest growing denomination in America and today boasts of many more members than any mainstream Protestant church in America. By and large it is composed of ordinary Americans guilty of nothing more than a yearning for transcendence in their lives.

Is this all so strange, their belief in the supernatural? According to a recent survey of the University of Chicago National Opinion Research Counsel, 29% of Americans have had visions of some sort, 42% have been in contact with the dead and 67% have experienced extrasensory perception.

Equally stalwart as Lillian McGlothin were other poor people on Mississippi Avenue, among them members of the Lewis-Herron-Swaggart-Gilley contingent.

About this religious sect with all its carryings-on, one matriarch today says, "We Methodists shouldn't have been so involved with our missionaries overseas; we should have done some missionary work on Mississippi Avenue instead."

One of Leona's rich and powerful helpers was again Mr. Corbett, who donated another of his lots for the church, this time on Texas Avenue. Another very rich and politically influential man, Lee Calhoun, went further and became emotionally as well as financially involved. Calhoun was a complex character who presented himself as uncouth, uneducated and poverty-stricken: a millionaire in torn jeans driving an old pickup truck. Yet he was descended from a distinguished family of lawyers and doctors who had migrated from South Carolina. He became rich as the owner of the many small farms he rented out in Ferriday, and he also owned land with abundant oil and natural gas resources. He added to this wealth by running Ferriday's main bootleg still. Related to the Swaggarts and the Lewises by marrying Stella Herron (sister of Jerry Lee Lewis', mother, Mamie, as well as Jimmy Swaggart's mother, Minnie Bell), he had a strong sense of *noblesse oblige* and was greatly given to openhanded generosity to his extended family. His early involvement with the Sumralls in their church revealed him to be just as eager to have his own soul saved as his poor relations were to save theirs.

A misconception about the Assemblies of God Church is that it is grim and humorless. In fact, its humor is as much an American commodity as its evangelism. If there is a note that is sounded consistently in Leona's history, it is that God, in his infinite wisdom, has quite a sense of humor. And she is never so unperceptive as to miss his jokes—even when she is the butt of them.

When Lee Calhoun, hard-headed businessman, first came to her apartment for a preliminary discussion of finances, where should he find her but emerging from under a bedsheet which served as a cloth on the kitchen table. "God a'mighty, woman, what are you doing under the table?" he exclaimed. Yet the next minute he accepted with equanimity Leona's flushed explanation that under the kitchen table was the only place she could find to shut herself in during her private conversations with God. Throughout their dealings with each other, each would be tolerant of the other's idiosyncrasies.

Calhoun did help enormously with both money and influence. But the family legend that he physically "built the church single-handed" has to be balanced against Leona's more accurate account of his sporadic activities. She tells of his happening by Texas Avenue one day, stopping to watch the workmen laying down the roof material for the church. All at once he decided to help. Placing a sheet of metal, he yelled "Nail it!" loud enough to be heard a block away. Then he began to sing at the top of his voice about living a holy life, shunning the wrong and doing the right, knowing that the Lord will make a way for him. Then he placed another sheet of material and yelled out, "Nail it!" And so it went until the end of the day when the roof was finished.

One night four strange men offered their services to Leona to work nights on the construction of the church. They worked hard and returned each night, also helping to build the small parsonage behind it. Every night they put money on the table for the hot chocolate and cookies the Sumralls provided. With construction completed, they mysteriously disappeared. Several months later it turned out they were part of the notorious recently captured Hairston Gang, wanted for robberies and killings, who had been hiding out just south of Ferriday. Apparently, they needed to get some exercise and fresh air.

A story Leona still recounts is that of finding a 200-pound man out cold on the floor of the church. The man had been praying out loud that he wanted the Lord to knock him out so he could feel His power. His prayers unanswered, the janitor nearby hit him as hard as he could "in Jesus' name."

Henry Herron (brother to Stella, Mamie and Minnie Bell) was a strong supporter with an unfortunately weak head for drink. Leona appointed him superintendent of the Sunday school, hoping to settle him down. One day his sister Stella ran to Leona spluttering s's: "Sister Sumrall, I hate to tell you but your Sunday school superintendent is standing down in front of Mr. Vogt's drugstore drunk." Taking it all in her stride, Leona arrived on the spot to help sober him up.

Built into the Assemblies of God is a stern exclusivity. Awful things happen to people who don't follow the path Leona instructed them in, who refuse to get saved in the approved manner. A woman who spread false, malicious rumors about the Sumralls had a son hit by a car, dying in a particularly ghastly way.

To be fair, awful things happened to people who *were* willing to get saved in her way. But God and Leona were always on hand to help them. She is particularly effective in deathbed conversions.

Congregation of
Assembly of God
Church in the late
1940's. Jerry Lee
Lewis is third row
left, next to Son
Swaggart and his
wife, Minnie Bell.
(*Credit: Gay Bradford
private collection.*)

In the early 1940's, the little white church had become part of Ferriday's church-going life, though its regular attendance would never be more than fifty members. Mission accomplished, for the Sumralls it was time to go on to more distant evangelistic fields. It was to be a long journey, but its end would be home in South Bend, Indiana, the base of brother Lester's ministry.

Leona, now Mrs. Leona Murphy, aged seventy, still preaches today. Her vocal delivery is flat, matter-of-fact, almost terse, with isolated moments of surprising tenderness. Her sermons contain certain humorous patches, most often when she is telling stories about the church she founded and pastored long ago in the small Louisiana town of Ferriday.

Throughout her stay in Ferriday, Leona remained true to her early promise of attracting the youth of the town. That she herself was still in her teens helped a great deal with the natural attraction of like to like. That she went out of her way personally to recruit them helped more.

The effect on one young couple she recruited, Son and Minnie Bell Swaggart, would have far-reaching effects, not only on them but unto the next generation and even the next. Back in that summer of 1936, Willie Leon Swaggart—forever called Son to distinguish him from his father, Willie Harry—worked late afternoons and evenings at a gas station within sight of the Sumralls' first open-air revivals. He was intrigued when he saw some of his mother's Herron relatives attending. He became more so when he heard the music and caught Leona's words. Night after night for what seemed like weeks, he found himself watching them.

Son was then a young man of twenty with a wife the same age as Leona and a year-old son named Jimmy. One day, to his surprise, the Sumralls came over to his house on Mississippi Avenue. They needed music and youth for their revivals, and the Swaggarts had both: Son being known locally for his fiddle and Minnie Bell for her singing and her guitar. Would they come with them and play at a prayer meeting seven miles up country? At this time, says Son, he was not a Christian and neither he nor his parents had ever been to a church a day in their lives. But he said yes because he was both curious and flattered. That marked the beginning of his turbulent up-and-down, in-and-out involvement with the Sumralls and the Assemblies of God. What began as a willingness to help out and an opportunity to play music (you might say he had been dragged in by his ears) grew into a kind of attachment to these strange meetings "where you never knew what might happen next," then turned into repudiation, and finally into surrender.

Perhaps the change going on inside him had really begun
the year before when he'd had a miraculous escape from jail.
He had been picked up by Federal agents, along with Jerry
Lee's father, Elmo, while working at what might be called
the family business, Uncle Lee Calhoun's moonshine still.
The men were loaded into a truck heading for internment
when Minnie Bell, seven months pregnant with Jimmy, came
running toward it. This sight so softened the agents that
they set Son free. Elmo was not so lucky. He was still in jail
when Jerry Lee was born. And neither were the five other
relatives so lucky. It made Son stop and think. Maybe it was
smarter to stay on the right side of the law. In fact, his
hairbreadth escape may have planted seeds in the lives of
both father and son. Father Swaggart, as lawless as any of
them, would develop interestingly in a suprising new direction.

Son from his beginnings was a driven man: driven from
the outset to make money.

By 1933, the interrelated, intermarrying clan of Lewises,
Herrons, Swaggarts and Gilleys had left Mangham, a farming
community in northern Louisiana, and come to Ferriday,
according to Son, for one reason only: to pick cotton. This
meant that they were dispossessed and desperate. They had
arrived at this state of affairs over what they now refer to
delicately as a "disagreement." With whom and over what
are lost in the mists of time. In those days of bank foreclo-
sures, of exhausted soil, of too many people fighting over too
few acres, over land rights, fishing rights and trapping rights,
bad blood could lead for these high-tempered people to
bloodshedding feuds with other clans or to clashes with the
law. Whatever the reasons for the "disagreement," its out-
come seems to have made it too hot for them to stay in
Mangham and they migrated to Ferriday, hoping to put defeat
behind them. For them it was a fresh start, turning over a
new leaf, putting their best foot forward. It should be noted
that in Ferriday, there is no record of them fighting with
anyone but themselves.

Besides picking cotton, the first thing Son did on arriving
in Ferriday, aged sixteen, was to go back to school, which he

had quit when he was fourteen. Most distinctly he recalls his teacher, Mrs. Waddell (of whom much more shall be learned in this history), who after a month told him straight out she didn't think he would pass any of his subjects. This made Son determined to prove her wrong, which he did. "She was a very strict teacher," he says, "but it was good to sit under her. She'd learn you something. After that she took an interest in me. I played fiddle and had a little band at the time, and she was very encouraging."

Son, however, having made his point, quit school in the middle of the ninth grade to get married. Back in Mangham he had come to know twelve-year-old Minnie Bell Herron, the sweet, cuddly baby of the family who had also moved to Ferriday. When they married, he had just turned eighteen and she sixteen. They did not live happily ever after. Jimmy Swaggart, in his autobiography *To Cross a River,* remembers a childhood with his parents continually fighting. Both high-tempered people, their shouting matches might end up with Minnie Bell alone and crying—or they might end up with her flinging their dinner out in the front yard. The family would subsequently have to gather up the meal.

By 1936, from early morning to late at night, Son was hard at work at various jobs. If he wasn't trapping animals—raccoon, possum, skunk and mink—he was curing them, stretching them, grading them and selling them to fur traders. In season he picked pecans, which he developed into a wholesale business. He also picked cotton and did some farming. Whenever he was free, he worked at the gas station in the afternoons and evenings. He did all this, of course, while also working at Calhoun's still and enjoying the consumption of its excellent liquor.

By the beginning of 1939, by dint of those American virtues of grit and guts, Son's various enterprises were beginning to pay off. Greed, another American virtue, overtook him. With his fur trapping and trading alone he would make, in season, $300 a day (the equivalent of $3,000 today)—more money in any year, says Son, than he has ever made since. However, during these years the Swaggarts were attending the Sumralls' meetings, which were having a curi-

ous effect on Son's conscience. Back in those days, Holiness
preachers, themselves always on the verge of poverty, made
it clear that you couldn't serve both God and Mammon. Son
felt the church holding him back. "I knew if I gave my heart
to the Lord and became a Christian, I wouldn't be able to
make the money I was making." This American dichotomy
is reflected throughout our history: Walden Pond versus
empire building, Woodstock versus Wall Street, hippies versus yuppies—the divided soul of America. When the conflict
became too painful, Son packed up his family, now consisting
of four-year-old Jimmy and six-month-old Donnie, and
headed for the Rio Grande area in Texas to strike it rich in
its vast agricultural opportunities.

Only two weeks later disaster struck: all the family came
down sick. Son and Donnie had pneumonia. In a drugstore
having a prescription filled for little Donnie, Son heard the
voice of God—"And I was just a sinner, and a lot of people
had said to me 'God don't speak to sinners.' Well, He spoke
to me and said, 'Your son is going to die,' and He said it three
times. There was no shouting, just an audible voice." Son,
for the first time in his life, broke down and cried. "When
something touches you hard enough, the tears is coming, you
see. I don't care who you are."

Back in Ferriday, the Sumralls had gone to Son's parents'
house to pray for the child and were confronted by what
sounds like a rehearsal for an Irish wake. All the Swaggart
relatives were drunk; one aunt was so drunk she had to hold
on to the furniture to walk. "Although I wanted to believe
that the boy would be healed, I just couldn't muster up much
hope because there was absolutely no faith in that home for
God to honor," Leona sternly records. Donnie died. As soon
as Son was well enough, they drove back to Ferriday.

By then the Assembly of God Church, though still in the
process of being completed, was holding its meetings on the
site. The Sumralls had organized a Sunday school and invited
visiting pastors. One of these was from Texas and had
recently lost a baby in Louisiana. Says Son, "It was vice
versa, see, we were from Louisiana, had lost our baby in
Texas." Yet he saw that the minister and his wife "held up

so good." The bereaved mother was always smiling. It put a question mark in Son's mind.

And there that question mark stayed until a few years later, when Son was saved at a revival preached by another visiting evangelist.

About his religious experience he has this to say: "The Lord had dealt mightily with me, and for two years I didn't have peace of mind. I was fighting something all the time, couldn't get away from it, couldn't outrun it. If I went yonder, it was over yonder. You see, I knew in my heart that I was the one who had caused God to take my child. Well, that's a heaviness and a guilt. And I knew, too, that I was the one holding my wife back because if I'd given my heart to the Lord two years previous, my wife would have too. And then all at once at that revival the guilt wasn't there. The heaviness wasn't there. Have you ever been concerned over something very much and then all at once you have a satisfied feeling about it? It's a relief, you see. A relief."

At that same revival, Minnie Bell and Son's father Willie Swaggart were saved, too; Son's formerly ailing mother, Ada, had been saved and healed several years back.

Now this is an interesting thing: right around the time that Son and Willie got saved—which coincided with the beginning of World War II—father Willie took a giant step in achieving the fear and respect of Ferriday by becoming its town marshall or police chief. Actually, he was the entire police force.

All during the war period and several years after, this wide-open town with its many bars and nightclubs was a popular hangout for soldiers stationed as far as fifty miles away. According to Jimmy Swaggart, only the heaviest drinkers got as far as Ferriday, and they were mean and tough. Before Willie had taken the job, you could hardly walk down the street without getting a beer bottle laid against your head. Yet the sight of this towering man mounted on his horse with his steel-cold gray eyes boring right through you was a sight fearsome and threatening enough to quell any rowdy strangers without his ever having to draw his pistol. As for Willie's style with his own townfolk, R. T. Bonnette, a journalist, remembers that one Christmas Eve Willie picked up a friend of Bonnette's who was out celebrating. This friend, it seems, had put a nickel in the jukebox at the Magnolia Hotel, and because he couldn't quite see, had pushed the wrong number. So he hauled off and kicked it. He was carrying on when old man Willie arrived and took him to jail. Bonnette followed them down there to ask what his friend was being charged with. "Reckless walking and talking," said Willie firmly.

Austin Wilson, a former oil contractor, talking about Willie's hands-on way with recalcitrant youngsters recalls that the old fellow knew what every boy in town was up to, and if he decided to take a belt to a kid, that boy wouldn't let his daddy know about it, because if he did, his daddy'd whip him, too.

Like his father, Son aspired to attain community dignity, thus putting him in another conflict with his church, which in those days could never by any stretch of imagination be called dignified. In fact, the particular evangelist who saved him had at first much offended Son and Minnie Bell with his emotional explosions. It was not so much that the citizens of Ferriday looked down on these activities as that they looked at them askance, getting high on booze being far more acceptable than getting high on the Holy Spirit.

However, children of all denominations loved the church. Hiram "Pete" Gregory, a professor of anthropology, says, "As a child I was raised a Catholic, but after mass I would run down to the Assembly of God Church. The Catholic services then were drab and somber and without music. At the Assembly of God there was always music, instruments, singing, always somebody with a guitar. The whole Mc-Glothin family could play and sing anything, and I grew up around them picking and singing."

Over the next years, Son, who never did anything by half-measures, felt the call to become a preacher growing stronger and stronger within him. He read the Bible, studied the word of God, went to Sunday school, turned up at the church whenever it was open and learned from the preachers—as in school days he had learned from Mrs. Waddell.

But whenever the subject came up, Minnie Bell, though herself an active churchworker, objected. By now they had a ten-acre truck farm and another child, Jeanette. Son also worked at a grocery store. They were doing well, most certainly in contrast to the preachers who they saw didn't even have the things they needed.

After two years of indecision, one night in 1945, Minnie Bell had a dream which Son remembers today in all its remarkable, Biblical imagery: an angel came and took Minnie Bell into heaven and showed her many things there. She walked down a great boulevard. The streets were gold. The mansions more beautiful than anything she had ever seen in her life, and all so real. At the end of the boulevard was a mansion half-finished, and the angel said, "This belongs to you." Minnie Bell asked why it was not finished, and the angel said, "I used all the materials you sent." Later they came to a big field where she saw piles of grain. "Minnie Bell," said the angel, "this is what your husband will do."

Son and Minnie Bell took this dream as seriously as any Jungian analyst, believing the symbols produced by the unconscious mind revealed ultimate truths that would guide them in their lives. That Minnie Bell's mansion was only half-finished she understood was because, in spite of all her services to the church, she was secretly in rebellion against the ministry itself. And as to the piles of grain in the field, Son explained that, to him, the field represented the world and the grain, the people. "It's like you plant grain out there and it fills the field." She understood what that meant, too.

"Honey," said Minnie Bell to Son, "I want you to be a preacher. We'll make out. We'll get by."

At the age of thirty-one, Son became a preacher, and in the course of his ministry built five churches, each of which he owned. It seems to have been God's will not to suppress his capitalist spirit—nor his fast-developing frugality.

Each profession has its shop talk. As a writer getting down to basics will measure his book by the number of copies sold, Son discusses his various parishes thus: "All the people in the church I built in Wisner were saved under our ministry. We had forty-nine saved in that church. I think

Son Swaggart, Jimmy's father, as preacher, circa 1949. (*Credit: Edna Gilley Mequet private collection.*)

only one Christian family was there when we came. In Vidalia, I built a very good promising church. I believe I was winning a hundred in about ten or eleven months on Sunday nights; that was considered pretty good."

From 1949 to 1962, he preached full time. His last church was in Baton Rouge.

━━━━━

On June 9, 1960, Minnie Bell died at forty-two after two operations, the first to have a goiter removed. Soon after, she had a hysterectomy and died on the operating table. Son blamed himself for allowing her to have this operation so quickly after the first. He went into shock and remained in that state for a year, not able to make daily decisions but still preaching. His family stood by, watching his horrible suffering, unable to help. In 1962, he gave up full-time preaching and returned to Ferriday, where he opened a furniture store and acquired four or five rent houses. From then to now he has preached at revivals. Since then he has been married twice, both times to women called Dorothy.

———

Recently one Sunday, he was preaching at the Assembly of God Church on Texas Avenue. He is a tall man with a straight, spare frame, nattily dressed in a summer jacket of a silvery gray and blue diamond pattern, a pale blue shirt, a silvery gray and pink tie, and well-tailored gray trousers. His slender, elegant feet were shod in the same expensive shoes that his son Jimmy sports.

Son's hair has faded to the pale color of silvery wheat. He wears horn-rimmed glasses. His seamed, drawn face, with its well-defined features, bears the look of someone shaken by universal thunder. When he began speaking, a familiar chord was struck, for his look was reminiscent of old Shakespearean actors who still toured England in the 1950's. These men also dedicated their lives to the retelling of our greatest stories, tugging on our strongest emotions—our basest as well as noblest—putting us in touch with more things in heaven and earth than we dream of. This comparison between the King James Bible-thumping evangelist and the barnstorming Shakespearean actor is not meant to be disparaging to either. They are both in daily contact with the glories of the Elizabethan language as well as the deep and awe-inspiring, centuries-old chronicles. Often, as in Son's case, that look of universal thunder is stamped on their features.

Son had returned only the night before from a twenty-nine-day-marathon revival in Kentucky—"I think the Lord could have won the battle in one day but the other twenty-eight made it sure"—and he was obviously exhausted. The middle-aged and elderly congregation was small, but he gave his all from the pulpit, as I suspect he always does.

His first thrust was euphoric. "We're going to have an old-fashioned, Holy Spirit revival!" he shouted. "God doesn't work in the negative! God did not create hell for man! He created hell for the devil!" Like any good preacher, he strides up and down, fully covering the stage, and in his clear enunciation of words, his sudden dead stops and perky turns of the head, there were eerie indications of his influence on the styles of both his preacher son Jimmy and his piano-playing nephew Jerry Lee Lewis.

His text was from Matthew 8:32. Just as Jesus in Gergesenes had cast the demons out into the herd of swine and the swine stampeded into the sea, carrying the demons along with them, where they all perished in the water, Son exorted the congregation to cast out sin settling down over Ferriday, bearing down on its rooftops and entering its houses. In your mind you see Sin slipping into the fast food restaurants that dot the main road and you wonder why the contemplation of sin in the abstract is such an enjoyable and invigorating exercise. And you marvel again how easily and neatly Jesus did for the people of Gergesenes what they could not do for themselves.

As he wound up his sermon, Son paused to put on his raincoat left on a nearby chair. He had gotten so overheated he needed to guard against chill. Then he picked up where he left off preaching, scarcely losing a beat. Finally, he invoked the Holy Spirit now moving in the church: "Things is happening tonight. I feel the breeze moving. The mulberry trees is moving. The spirit is moving." At the end of the service his face was drained white, then flushed pink as the blood came through his thin, time-worn skin.

Claudia Cooper, a large woman with a pretty face and a thrilling voice, sang, "Flow through me, Holy Spirit. Move through me, love through me." There was praying out loud from the congregation, some speaking in tongues. There was crying also and the box of Kleenex on the table under the pulpit was used.

Then all joined hands in a circle and said the Lord's Prayer and the service was over.

A BRIEF INTRODUCTION
TO SOME OF THE PLAYERS

The year 1936, when Leona came to Ferriday, was a historically explosive year. It is a year to pause at and consider
closely, not only what was going on on Mississippi Avenue in
Ferriday, but what was going on globally. It was the year that
the winds of change tore up and down and around the world,
racing and roaring and raging into every corner, however
hidden or obscure.

Gone with the Wind, published that year, could serve as
an apt title as well for the many things that went windward,
not least being the desperate hope that World War I had
been "the war to end war." When civil war broke out in
Spain in July of that year, it was called by doom-sayers (who
happened in this instance to be right) the curtain rising on
World War II in the West. When China declared war on
Japan in December, it was called the curtain rising on World
War II in the East.

That year in November came Hitler and Mussolini's
proclamation of the Rome-Berlin Axis, which would sound—
as it was no doubt intended to—as if the very axis of the

globe had changed direction and was spinning the opposite way.

It was a tense world, a world with names in the news that would live on in history: Hitler, Mussolini, Franco, Chiang Kai-shek. Roosevelt was re-elected by a landslide, and Churchill, leading His Majesty's loyal opposition, made memorable speeches sounding the alarm as German troops occupied the Rhineland.

Here and there in that year rockets were set off that would illuminate our future. Two print revolutions took place. In America, Henry Luce published the first issue of *Life* magazine, inaugurating the revolution of photojournalism. In England, another publishing revolution was initiated, the paperback one, begun by Allen Lane with his Penguin paperback series of good books at sixpence each, thus enabling readers to be enlightened for a price they could afford.

Another revolution in communications also took place. That year, in England, the British Broadcasting Company inaugurated the first television service in any country.

The year opened with King George V of England dying and being succeeded by his popular son, Edward VIII, who stepped up to the throne and then, in an unprecedented move, stepped down again to abdicate eleven months later for the woman he loved. The story of this former king, who would become the Duke of Windsor, marrying the American divorcée Wallis Simpson would seem on the surface to have had all the elements of making it the romance of the century. But it wasn't. Curiously, what did become the romance of the century showed up that same year in the persons of Rhett and Scarlett, the fictitious lovers who have since become part of our lives more than any who actually lived.

And two significant journeys into the human psyche were made public by two significant men: the first by Freud in his *Autobiography*, which revealed how his psyche had been put together; the second by F. Scott Fitzgerald in *The Crack-up*, revealing how his psyche had fallen apart.

This bumper year of 1936 is a good year to find out what a curious assortment of well-known people were up to—people who spent either their early, middle or late years in Ferriday and its environs (the town serving as main town, where-you-spend-your-money town, market and merchandise town, black music town, railroad town and Saturday-night town for the twenty miles of farming communities surrounding it). For this obscure corner of the earth—this infinitesimal, not to say nonexistent, dot on the map, this tiny upstart town, which only came into existence in 1903—claims to have produced more famous people per square mile than any other small town. What follows is a brief introduction to some of these lives, which will be more fully explored in their proper places.

Two men in particular, Howard K. Smith and General Claire Lee Chennault, the one born in, the other who would come later to this dot, deserve first mention, as both will be taking leading roles in the even more earth-shattering events to come in the next years: Smith by reporting these events and Chennault by making them. For both of them this year would be pivotal.

General Chennault, born in 1893 in Commerce, Texas, shortly thereafter moved with his family to a farm some forty miles from Ferriday in a town called Gilbert. At seventeen, he married his first wife, Nell Thompson, from Waterproof, and he would build his house on Ferriday's Lake St. John. For the tough, scarfaced, half-deaf, ex-barnstorming pilot forty-three-year-old Captain Chennault of the regular Army Air Force, 1936 would mark the year in which his life as he knew it was over. The year had not begun badly. In January, he took a spectacular part in the Pan American Air Maneuvers in Miami. With two other expert flyers trained by him, he was demonstrating his "Three Men on a Flying Trapeze" act. Flying P-12s, they smoothly executed sensational stunts. Twenty-foot lengths of light rope tied the planes together to ensure that all the acrobatics—the loops, chandelles, Immelmanns, slow rolls and double rolls—were done in perfect unison for the amazement of the spectators. Chennault, however, had a serious purpose behind this display. It was to demonstrate yet again his long-held theory—held, it must be said, in violent opposition to official Air Force policy—of the superiority of three fighter planes flying in strict formation in combat to intercept and destroy enemy planes more effectively than the lone heavily armed bombers which the Air Force was committed to. If the Army was fed up with "that radical Chennault and his crackbrain schemes," there was a spectator in the crowd who was not. He was General Mow Pang Tsu of the China air force, and he told Chennault how much he was impressed with him, his theories and the manner in which he presented them. They were destined to meet again under far different circumstances.

Chennault spent the rest of that winter uncharacteristically flat on his back in a hospital bed in Hot Springs, Arkansas. His health was failing; he was suffering from chronic bronchitis and exhaustion. Forced to take stock of his situation, he conceded that the future looked grim. His army rank was captain, as it had been for many years, and he had no hope of promotion. The Air Force brass had no use for the stubborn, argumentative man. When Army doctors found his hearing impaired (although he was no deafer than any other flyer who flew in noisy, open cockpits), the brass seized on this and "suggested" he retire. Though his official separation from the Army would not be finalized until the next year, Chennault had already accepted defeat.

Leaving the hospital in spring, he went on sick leave back home to his cottage on Lake St. John where he lived with his first wife, Nell, and their eight children. From there that summer he was often seen stunt flying over Coola Cusa, a large house on the lake that had been turned into a dance pavilion on the water. Old-timers like Blanche Chauvin and R. T. Bonnette tell of watching Chennault perform his flying trapeze act with two other pilots as well as his solo acrobatics. He also took Ferridians up in his airplane for a thrill during the Mississippi Regatta. For the rest of the time he did what he had always done from childhood on. He hunted and he fished. And, still at work on his pursuit flying theories and ways to prove them, he thought and he wrote. Unfortunately, he knew, it would require a war to put them into practice.

Soon after his release from the hospital he had received, in a letter, a startling offer from Madame Chiang Kai-shek herself to come to China and confidentially inspect its air force. Should he take up her offer or not? He kept turning it over in his mind.

When China declared war on Japan at the end of 1936, he had made his decision. Five months later, on April 30th, he received his final Army discharge papers. On the following day, he left Louisiana and boarded a ship from San Francisco bound for China, taking a step that would totally and irrevocably alter the course of his life.

In 1936, it would seem to Howard K. Smith, in contrast to Chennault, that his life was just beginning. Born in September 1914, right on Main Street (now called Louisiana Avenue) in Ferriday, he, along with Edward R. Murrow and Eric Sevareid in the 1930's, was to shape for years to come our concept of the news commentator, first on radio and then on TV. Now, more than fifty years later, this scholarly pundit, outspoken and uncompromising, is still confounding both critics and admirers with his unpredictable commentaries on all subjects.

In Ferriday's infancy, Howard's mother and father had moved from the neighboring parish of Pointe Coupée in search of the kind of livelihood his father could only obtain there. Due to financial reverses his father was not pursuing a gentlemanly profession or a gentlemanly vocation or even a gentlemanly trade, but what some people would consider just a plain old job.

May of 1936 found Howard K. Smith, Jr., aged twenty-one, in New Orleans. A history major, he had just graduated from Tulane with top honors. He had applied for a Rhodes scholarship at Oxford, but in order to be eligible he needed one extra credit. From his freshman year Howard's eye had been on Germany and the rise of Hitler. He already had two years of German as his foreign language ("To this day," says his wife, "he still speaks it with a southern accent."). Therefore, he decided to get the credit by taking a summer course at Heidelberg University. "Heidelberg," he says, "had these Nazi-type scholarships. They wanted anybody, especially any young American, they could get. The curriculum was German language in the morning, and what turned out to be propaganda lectures in the afternoon."

He had sold a short story for a hundred dollars, and with ten dollars for a passport, he had ninety dollars left for this adventure. He took a freighter to Bremen, working his way over as a deckhand. Before his studies began, he spent his time touring Germany. What he saw appalled him. Rarely in his life had Howard seen anyone in uniform who wasn't a Boy Scout. In Nazi Germany he went through towns where every fourth man was in uniform. He saw tanks, cannons, war trucks, anti-aircraft guns on the move. "Steel-helmeted men from Mars held up traffic crossing streets." In Nuremberg he watched a river of 20,000 men in uniform goose-stepping. "If there's going to be war," thought young Howard, "I could become a foreign correspondent."

By the time he left Germany two months later, he felt it a threat to the existence of any civilization compatible with his values. Interestingly, he would uphold these values for the rest of his life. These values contained words like *reason, think, discuss* and *fact,* instead of the Nazi's *hate, obey* and *fight.* From this base would grow the man chosen to moderate the first presidential TV debate.

Howard's afternoon propaganda lectures at Heidelberg did not, as was their aim, succeed in making him love Germany but had the opposite effect of scaring him to death. In his book *Last Train from Berlin,* he describes, by reason and fact, the steps he took to reach his youthful but accurate conclusion: "Nazism absolutely and necessarily meant war."

He returned at the end of the summer bursting with a desire to tell the world what he had seen. For several months he worked for a New Orleans newspaper rewriting dispatches from foreign news agencies and writing on foreign affairs and Germany. Ahead for him was another return to Germany, followed by a Rhodes scholarship at Oxford. For Howard, the year 1936 had set the course of his life.

Up the Mississippi River since the beginning of its settlement came Jews and Italians to small river towns as they sprang into existence. The Italians went into the restaurant and grocery businesses, and the Jews into dry goods and hardware. One Jewish family who had early settled in Ferriday was the large Pasternack family consisting of Wolf, the patriarch, and his many sons. With them and especially with his eldest, Joe, he created a hardware and dry goods store the like of which had not been seen, and it would become famous all over Louisiana. They named it, of course, Pasternacks. Built on soaring aspirations, the store became for them an entree into diversified business enterprises and investments, which would make them, in Ferriday's favorite phrase, "millionaires many times over." In local newspapers, Wolf and Joe would be referred to as merchant princes. They would also become town benefactors. Their wide-flung political influence and money would help build roads and levees. In fact, Wolf and Joe so wove themselves into the fabric of the town that they emerged as its most necessary economic mainstay.

In 1936, when Ferriday was still foundering in the depths of the Depression, Pasternacks, now under the leadership of Joe, instead of retrenching to curtail its losses, held fast and extended credit to the townspeople. This show of loyalty and faith would pay off in many ways. Joe Pasternack loved show business and one of his most oft-repeated expressions was that "the show must go on." Having survived major floods of the teens and twenties that inundated the town, he was not going to be deterred by a spot of bother called the Depression.

They must have been concerned, however, as were Jews all over America at the time, at the virulent winds of anti-Semitism that swept the nation in the thirties.

━━━━━

Mrs. U. B. "Jo" Evans—Jo N. Evans—is a most remarkable woman. A renowned horticulturist and archeologist, she has lived on her plantation, Haphazard, for some fifty years. She is actively involved in every aspect of the town. A steel magnolia of sturdiest bloom, she has been able, by the superiority of her mind, the many facets of her talent and a strongly communicative personality, to juggle with consummate ease such diverse things as Bradford ornamental pear trees and Louisiana politics.

By 1936, Mrs. Evans and her husband had pinpointed their decision to buy a plantation and were turning their eyes toward one of the richest agricultural regions in Louisiana, which, it so happened, had Ferriday as its main town.

———

Among the black citizens of Ferriday today is the blues trombonist Peewee Whittaker, who has made the town his home for over thirty years. "I am the best and oldest trombone player living," he recently stated to me, "I am ninety-two years and three weeks old." His story is the whole history of black Southern musicians in the twentieth century. His reminiscences are invaluable. Regional recognition all over northeast Louisiana Peewee has always had. Now he is getting worldwide recognition.

Peewee Whittaker has been a working musician for over seventy years. In the early 1930's, Peewee had been playing in a large band doing prestigious gigs on a circuit that included Louisiana, Arkansas and Mississippi, recognized as America's musically creative heartland. Yet in 1936, he suddenly left the band to tour with F. S. Wolcott's Rabbit's Foot Minstrels. His next fifteen years were spent playing trombone in circus and carnival bands as well as in minstrel shows.

What enabled Peewee to go from job to job was that, as a good reading musician as well as a musician able to play two or three other instruments, he was always in demand and easily got jobs not offered to musicians who could not read. These musical illiterates he still deprecates, referring to them as "bump-de-bump players," and scorning their "faking" and "juking."

Peewee settled down permanently in Ferriday in 1954, drawn by the girls. They were fast, he said, and he liked that. Living in Ferriday meant being the house band for

Haney's famous Big House, where all the important black stars performed.

It almost seems to be the rule that in order to attain excellence, bluesmen must be excessively romantic, sexually active and believe every word of every love song that celebrates the crucialities and casualties of the heart. For this is the stuff, these raw emotions, that black music has always used to build its shimmering, glimmering, sleepless kingdom that at some time has held us all in its thrall, whether—to borrow a phrase from Peewee—we are black as midnight or white as twelve o'clock in the day.

In Ferriday, there was a young white kid whom Peewee got to know quite well. At Haney's Big House Peewee let Jerry Lee Lewis sit in with his band. According to him, "[Jerry Lee] would ask for ideas and I'd show him. I just showed him how to stop and take his time and all like that."

In 1936, Jerry Lee Lewis and his cousin, Jimmy Swaggart, were both only one year old, while his other cousin, Mickey Gilley, had been born in March of that year. For now it need only be pointed out that these infants, who would later carve careers for themselves in evangelism, in rock and in country music, who would achieve world fame and infamy, were the products of their parents' vaulting ambitions, parents who would do everything in their power to see that their sons had a better life than their own cotton-picking past. The dynamics of this interrelated family, all living closely together, had begun and would explode into action with the coming of Leona and the Assembly of God.

Unquestionably, what this group of people all have in common is that they are all passionate communicators or more accurately, *communicants*, early in touch with something beyond their everyday existence, with some inner conviction that would last all their lives. It is as if something inside them was fairly screaming to be let out, as if, metaphorically, each is grabbing you by the lapels saying, "Listen to me. Hear what I have to tell you. It will change your life. It will change the world." Although these people appear to turn up precisely when needed, they were none of them merely filling someone else's shoes. They were instead pushing, striving, enduring and prevailing to make themselves heard, to make themselves known, in short, to get their own way.

Ferriday was always a permissive town, basically a live-and-let-live town, though in its past on Saturday nights it could also be called a live-and-let-die town. From its earliest days, it has been a culturally complex community which includes not only Jews, Italians and blacks, but Chinese and Mexicans as well as white Protestants. Ferriday made them think and feel differently from other more homogeneous small towns in the South. It has accepted people's differences, yet it is far from complacent, for, to keep things hopping, it is also where back-country fundamentalist morality clashes with free-and-easy Mississippi River morality.

NATCHEZ

When Leona Sumrall went downriver to Ferriday in Concordia Parish to unearth her jewels and valuable treasures by founding a church, she was seeking her own salvation through the worship of her God. Some 130 years before her, in 1798, a Spaniard, Don Jose Vidal, went from Natchez directly across the Mississippi River (some three-quarters of a mile wide at that point) to unearth *his* jewels and treasures by founding Concordia Parish. He too was seeking his own salvation through the worship of his God—property. Although for both of them everything seemed primed, even preordained for their arrival on our particular dot in this area of northeast Louisiana, both must be seen as also responding to cosmic events beyond their control.

What in the annals of history led Don Jose Vidal to just that place at just that time? And what steps did he himself take to arrive?

History, we are told, has many cunning passages yet none so cunning, convoluted, complicated and confusing as the history of the Louisiana Territory, beginning in 1682, when the explorer La Salle claimed and named it for France's Louis XIV. The claim included not only both sides of the Mississippi, but a very great deal of the rest of America. In a solemn ceremony, La Salle validated the takeover by stating it was done "with the consent of the Natchez Indians."

The district, where dwelled the Natchez nation in their sacred village high on the cliffs and bluffs of the east bank of the Mississippi, remained empty of white settlement until the early 1700's. When a French expedition came up the river and chose this beautiful spot well above the malarial swamps of the vicinity as a strategic place to settle, they established a military post called Fort Rosalie on its cliffs. Then followed the clash of white settlers and Indians, facing each other in mounting discord. Hostile incidents followed one after another, quickening the proud Indian sense of outrage that a treaty with the white man was one thing, harsh treatment by them, another. Events exploded in 1729. The Indian massacre of the French fort was one of the bloodiest episodes of the era. The French retaliated and with the aid of their allies, the Choctaws, wiped out most of the Natchez nation. Some of the survivors were sold into slavery. The majority of the rest dispersed. So horrendous and bloody was the slaughter that for the next thirty years Indian spirits would be said to haunt the desecrated area, and only a scattering of French settlers were foolhardy enough to stay in the forbidding miasma of its atmosphere. Over in France, these spirits would also haunt the writer Chateaubriand, so firing his romantic imagination that, without setting foot on the American continent, he would immortalize the proud nation as the noble savages of his novel *Les Natchez*.

In 1762, France, exhausted by the seven-year war with England over Canada, was forced into a giving vein. In a secret treaty, Louis XV made a gift of all the Louisiana Territory east of the Mississippi to his Spanish cousin, Charles III. Secret treaties, in which the people on the spot who are most concerned have no say in the matter of what country they are to be governed by, don't work. As the news slowly leaked to New Orleans, the French Governor Charles Aubry expressed his agitation thus: "I am in one of the most extraordinary positions. I command for the King of France, and at the same time I govern the colony as if it belonged to the King of Spain."

When his high-handed gift of themselves to Spain finally became public knowledge to the colonists in 1768, the French, German and Acadian settlers, finding it a threat to their existence, banded together, took up arms and rebelled. It was the first self-determined insurrection in America. Its numbers were small and the duration of independence brief. The rebellion was put down by an Irishman, Captain-General Alejandro O'Reilly of the Spanish army. But Louisiana had taken a step no other American colony had yet taken. The issues of these people determined to have a say in their own government would come to the fore again when, by another secret treaty in 1800, Spain gave Louisiana back to France, and yet once more in 1803, when President Thomas Jefferson purchased their country out from under them.

━━━

The year after Louis XV gave the region west of the Mississippi to Spain, he ceded to England—this time in open treaty—its east bank, which included Natchez.

If the French were wary of Natchez, the British were delighted with it, so delighted that they referred to it as "the Fourteenth Colony." They stayed delighted for sixteen years, from 1763 to 1779. Englishmen writing from there spoke glowingly of the rich fertility of this Delta land compared to the "barren deserts of Canada and Florida." When the American Revolution erupted, Natchez became a refuge for the English fleeing from the other crown colonies.

With the arrival of the English, Natchez became like a Merry Widow or, rather, a Gay Divorcée (always in the background there is music and dancing), who changes partners often, each time doing a little better for herself, as she did when she turned to them from the beleaguered French. The English treated her with pomp and circumstance, cultivating her rich land with plantations, encouraging her flirtatiousness with cotillions, developing in her a taste for privilege, snobbery, fine china and family portraits. They loved her—but they couldn't keep her; which is not to say that, with plots and plans, they never stopped trying to get her back. Without doubt, Natchez had "It." Metamorphically, she was telluric—the term physicists give to a place when the electric currents flowing beneath its surface are unnaturally high.

Though the American War of Independence was being fought and won (in the ebullient spirit of '76, a Captain Gibson even managed briefly to hoist the American flag over its fort), it was not to these bold young Americans but to the sophisticated, worldy seductions of the Spanish she yielded, particularly to the fascinations of Don Manuel Gayoso de Lemos. As her Governor from 1789 to 1797, highly cultivated and fluent in English, Gayoso taught her how to rule over her predominantly Anglo-American subjects with a mixture of good works, exquisite manners, tolerance, intrigue and conspiracy. He gave her an even more lavish lifestyle, laying out her streets, building a hospital which took in charity cases, including Indians, and financing the popular race track, Fleetfield. Under his guidance, she became so telluric that her population tripled. It was the beginning of her tradition of sumptuous antebellum mansions, from which the tradition of conversation as an art became a habit that spread to all her economic classes.

Governor Gayoso named his magnificent residence, the center of political and social life, "Concord" to celebrate the amity that existed between the English-speaking settlers of the Natchez District and their Spanish rulers. The gesture was heartfelt as well as diplomatic. Gayoso's devoted right-hand man Don Jose Vidal was to invoke this spirit when he named the post on the east bank of the river "Concord," and, by extension, the surrounding land "New Concordia," out of which came present day Concordia Parish.

Yet underneath all this concord was continuing discord. During Gayoso's rule as well as immediately after, a positive shower of mutually contradictory treaties between the English and Spanish, the Americans and Spanish, the Americans and English, the Spanish and French, and the Americans and French rained down upon her.

Gayoso saw his political task of keeping Natchez for his own as threefold: first, to stymie the English plot to invade her from Canada; second, to frustrate the French Jacobins' plan to retake Louisiana and then march on Natchez and third, even to thwart a Spanish-American treaty of 1795 which turned her over to the Americans. Spain may have given up on Natchez, but Gayoso—never! By the use of all kinds of delaying tactics, he hoped to make this treaty a dead letter, for he had reason to believe that the loose confederacy of states would fall apart and because of this he headed up an interesting intrigue that was called the Spanish Conspiracy by those in the know. Kentucky and Tennessee were far from happy at being designated states. These Westerners hated the ruling Eastern establishment and wanted to be independent of it. Gayoso was especially welcoming to people from those states, both traders and settlers, who came to Natchez, and he even made trips to Kentucky to woo it into the Spanish fold.

To implement this conspiracy, Gayoso needed a number of co-conspirators and spies to check with him regularly at his court—and he got them. They were of all nationalities: some were U.S. citizens, some English, some Spanish, some Irish—and some were involved in other conspiracies. It is astonishing how many prominent men in the early throes of democracy wore coats of many colors. But always the man most directly in his confidence was his trustworthy servant Don Jose Vidal who, as second-in-command, acted as Governor when Gayoso was away from home.

This Spanish conspiracy did not, of course, succeed. It was to be neither America's nor Natchez's destiny. But even after it failed and Gayoso was forced to relinquish his beloved Natchez to the arms of the importunate young Republic, Spain had found him so effective that his next post, a decided step up, was as Governor General of New Orleans, which office he took over in 1797.

Could he have died there two years later of a broken

heart? Actually, he died of yellow fever, but at the time, unkind rumor had it that the real cause of his death was his drinking bouts with his old friend and co-conspirator General James Wilkinson, the devious turnabout self-styled "George Washington of the West," for many years a Spanish agent. Heavy on his heart had also been the necessity of selling his home, Concord, for his multitudinous activities had left him heavily in debt.

Captain Don Jose Vidal, who becomes in the march of history "Josef" and then "Joseph" Vidal, is, in contrast to Gayoso, an elusive figure. Is he enigmatic or simply dull? The pages of history where he keeps turning up seem almost determined to present him without interest. The closest to a character assessment of him that can be found is by the historian John F. H. Claiborne, who knew him, and it sounds more like a funeral oration:

"He had all the characteristics of the Spanish gentle-man—proud, ceremonious, dignified but generous, hospita-ble, ever ready to confer a favor."

What have we here? Perfect casting for the perfect private secretary? Or the perfect attendant lord to the ruling prince?

To explain Vidal's further actions, further facts are needed. And finally, after pages of Gayoso and Vidal linked together in ceremonial duties, we find him on his own at last as "a well-to-do Captain in the Spanish army who speculated heavily in real estate in Natchez and later what was to become Concordia." This separates him not only from Gayoso but other Spanish officials in that part of the country. For the odd thing was that the aristocratic Spanish rulers wished to rule but not to settle.

Originally from Galicia, the same part of Spain as Gayoso, Vidal was also accepted into the highest Natchez society. From his actions it can be deduced that the acquisition of property was for him his deliverance, his redemption, his deepest belief. He made sound provisions for his sons to become landowners. He masterminded his daughter Maria's marriage to Samuel Davis, originally of Philadelphia, Penn-sylvania, who, under Vidal's guidance, became a prosperous landowner in Concordia. He even saw to it that his sister married another landowner, Thomas Thompson, whose early exclusive ferry franchise across the river became a family affair, and that his brother, a priest, would pastor the Catholic community in Concordia Parish. He was, in short, a good family man. In history books, one touch of sentimentality breaks through the implacable dignity of Vidal's facade: when his wife, Jacinda, dies, he buries her high on the Natchez bluff so that from his new home in Concordia, the sun's rays outlines her grave for him every day.

This same sun had set on the Spanish regime in Natchez. When Gayoso left Natchez in the summer of 1797, he made Vidal interim Commandant of the Post. However, with the immediate arrival of the American military and the departure of the Spanish military, it took no more than a few skirmishes with the new regime in 1798 for Vidal to see how hollow this title actually was. Land speculators who intend to stay well-to-do must act decisively. Early in March, Vidal fired off a petition to his former boss which said it all: as the United States is taking possession of Natchez, he wished to remove into Spanish Territory (Louisiana). Calling Gayoso's attention to the vacant land on the west side of the Mississippi opposite Natchez, he prayed for a grant of 800 arpents (equal to about 680 acres) for himself and 500 arpents (or 425 acres) for each of his sons.

Shortly, Gayoso answered his prayer, stipulating only that twenty arpents (seventeen acres) be reserved for a fort to be built to provide a place of refuge *"for reputable persons living east of the River who might not want to remain there."* (my italics)

Vidal got his land surveyed and planned his move. A number of the other pro-Spanish people from Natchez, missing the halcyon days of Gayoso's government, gave up their homes to follow Vidal's lead to the Spanish Territory of Concordia though they never had to huddle in the fort to escape the Americans. The Louisiana Purchase was but a few years away. Had the Spaniard Vidal dallied or delayed, there would be no Vidalia and no Concordia Parish—at least not by these names. It is a nice irony that, though Vidal was not, in the end, to escape the push westward of the young

Republic, he had by his perspicacity secured himself a place in it.

With Gayoso's death, the formal end to Spanish rule in all this territory was only one year away. As previously mentioned, in 1800, a secret treaty between the Spanish King and Napoleon gave Louisiana to the French. And three years later, of course, Napoleon sold it to Jefferson. Laussat, the French colonial prefect in New Orleans, hearing the rumor a month after the fact, promptly branded the Louisiana Purchase "an incredible, impudent lie." Loyalties, land grants and land purchases were all mixed up for quite some time to come in a veritable black comedy of errors.

Given its history, Louisiana's reluctance at being annexed by the United States in 1812 is understandable. In fact, the Constitutional Convention in New Orleans that year held to admit Louisiana into the Union had two delegates from Concordia Parish who opposed the resolution on grounds of the differences of race, customs and language of the inhabitants, though they finally gave in.

Louisiana to this day remains stubbornly itself and stubbornly different from the rest of the states. Where the rest of them are divided into counties, Louisiana divides itself into parishes. Its laws are based on the Napoleonic Code instead of English common law. Instead of county supervisors, the same body of governors is given the stop-look-and-listen name of "police jury." Its large population of Acadians (Cajuns) still stubbornly speak French, though they have been in America for over 200 years.

———

Concordia Parish became a Gateway to the West. Along the trails formerly used by cattle and horse traders, the new Americans came in great numbers by horse, by covered wagon and, for some, by very stately carriage. The west these pioneers were about to create was not only the wild west but the homely linsey-woolsey west and the west of already substantial landowners who wanted more.

Vidal was the right person for his time. Whether he understood himself or not, this loyal Spaniard was an American, which is why he succeeded and the charismatic Gayoso failed. The difference between these men was the difference between the *ancien regime* and the new, between the European aristocrat and the American entrepreneur who would settle down and make the land his own. Gayoso's need for personal glory was always connected with the glory of Spain. Vidal felt little need for personal glory—just personal property.

In 1811, Vidal's modest bid for immortality was satisfied by having the first little town in Concordia Parish named Vidalia in his honor for his having laid out the streets and donating part of his own land for such municipal uses as a courthouse and a school. Born in 1765, Vidal died in his sixties, a long life for that time. On his death in 1828, he was buried in the plot of his Davis descendants.

———

Like Vidal himself, Vidalia became a staid town, certainly compared to her neighboring upstart Ferriday, which from its inception was a town with a bad reputation. However, as there is no reputable town that does not have its disreputable side, so Vidalia in the 1800's was known, according to Alonzo Smith, the famous cattle driver, as "one of the toughest little towns in the world." It was in Vidalia that cowboys, having sold their cattle in Natchez, were paid off, and they celebrated in saloons, dance halls and gambling houses.

Another interesting aspect to the duality of Vidalia was a series of events quite out of the ordinary that took place on its sandbar. But since these events began in Natchez, let us return to her to see how she's doing under the Americans.

With huge plantations and ever more elaborately elegant homes, opera houses and theaters as well as race tracks, Natchez might be said to be living higher and higher on the hog, until she rivaled only New Orleans in the entire South for her architectural beauty, her millionaires, her easy morality, her ostentation—and her decadence.

The first half of the nineteenth century was an excitable time for her, and she produced some very excitable citizens to match. Although she was isolated from the main centers of power, which were on the eastern seaboard, she was unusually alert to national issues, about which these excitable citizens held passionate but distinctly divergent views. Many wars were being fought during this time that were deemed necessary for the United States' survival—against the English in New Orleans, the Indians in Alabama and Florida, the Mexicans in Texas and the Mexicans in Mexico—in which many Natchez men became eager participants.

It was during this period that a rash of dueling broke out. It spread like a fashionable epidemic, infecting only her most distinguished inhabitants who felt perceived insults to their honor. It was as if one man bumped against another, causing great bruises of insult to rise, festering inside them until the only possible antidote was pistols at dawn. The favorite dueling ground was the sandbar at Vidalia.

Like Ferriday after it, Natchez was permissively not only a live-and-let-live town, but a live-and-let-die town. Where Ferriday had Saturday night shoot-outs, spurred in the heat of the moment by drink, Natchez's fights were more sophisticated, more polished. Dueling went on for a long time—in spite of strong laws against it—in fact, right up until the Civil War. If you were a stranger in town, or rather a highly distinguished stranger, you had better be careful before opening your mouth, because words could kill.

A lot of high-flown talk surrounded these duels, talk about chivalry and the cavalier code, and knight-errants and vindicating one's personal honor, but perhaps the last word goes to the University of Mississippi's *Encyclopedia of Southern Culture*:

> Prime evidence for this [Southern addiction to violence] was the duel which became widely accepted among "gentlemen" in the South whereas it died out soon after its introduction in the North . . . the duel was the most formalized means of defending an exaggerated sense of honor with violence.

Who exactly were these men who adorned themselves with this exaggerated sense of honor? Many were in the military, though you would have thought that, active as they were in all the ongoing wars, they would not be averse to a bit of peace and quiet while on leave. Politicians fought duels, as did judges, lawyers, and newspaper editors—a scrappy lot. But that doctors fought duels as well seems ironic, for surely they are under the Hippocratic oath to save lives.

What actually transpired at these sandbar duels was that no sooner had the first shots been fired when all concerned, duelists and seconds and good friends, behaved in a way that was anything but gentlemanly.

In 1806, a Major Claiborne and a Captain Farar fought a duel. They fired their shots and both men ended up alive. But immediately afterward, a friend of Farar's turned upon Claiborne violently, insisting that Claiborne fight him as well. Claiborne refused and there followed lengthy lectures on dueling etiquette.

In 1811, George Poindexter, Attorney General of Mississippi, challenged a rich merchant, Abidjah Hunt, to a duel for "making slighting remarks about Thomas Jefferson." The duel was fought and Hunt was killed. End of the affair? Not at all. Poindexter was publicly accused by the Hunt faction of firing *before* the word "fire." It was the cause of endless pronouncements and squabbling thereafter.

In 1810, a young captain, Winfield Scott, who would become a famous general, was challenged to a duel by Doctor Upshaw for speaking disrespectfully of his superior, who turned out to be none other than our slippery old friend General James Wilkinson. They went about their business and both ended up alive without post-duel incident, but the duel did help Scott in a court martial that followed because it proved "he was a man of honor."

One fight, celebrated to this day, took place in 1827 and became known as the Sandbar Fight. It was, in fact, less a duel than a mini-war with twelve angry men, six on either side, including prominent doctors and generals as well as seconds and well wishers. Dr. Thomas Maddox faced the planter Colonel Samuel Wells, the quarrel originating, as Dr. Maddox explained later, "over some cause that I do not recollect at this time." The leading players squared off and both rounds fired missed their marks. The combatants shook hands, considered their honor satisfied and went off to share a convivial glass of wine. Then came the post-duel debacle. Two other men of the party decided it was time to settle their own differences. Then others found that they, too, had serious grievances. Two men ended up dead—one a general— and two were badly wounded. James Bowie, of Bowie knife fame, though himself seriously wounded, nevertheless got to kill his old enemy Sheriff Norris Wright by wielding the "awesome blade of his design." This free-for-all is said to be the first public use of the Bowie knife. Every year, around the time of the Sandbar Fight, there is a James Bowie Festival at Taconey House (Vidal's home) sponsored by the Vidalia Chamber of Commerce. Demonstrations of Bowie knives are held. One man dresses as James Bowie in a white hat. Around 12,000 people attend.

The Sandbar Fight inaugurated a wild four-year period of dueling in Natchez. The arguments leading to the duels always seemed less important than the opportunity they afforded to play this exclusive high-risk game. An argument, for instance, over the residence requirements for voting in 1828 seemed a fair enough reason for two grown men to try and kill each other. And always there would be an unpleasant aftermath with men accusing one another of violating some article of the code duello.

One duel emerging from Vidalia itself bears looking into. In 1841, a district judge was presiding over a separation suit that a woman brought against her husband. The irate husband challenged the judge to a duel and killed him. Thus was justice served.

As for Natchez herself, she simply looked the other way at these private wars—boys, after all, will be boys. She was good at rising above things, detaching herself from the hurly-burly, and like Paris, always thinking first and last of her own beauty and how to preserve it. She had remained neutral during the American Revolution and, though unquestionably Southern, she would remain neutral during the Civil War, even graciously welcoming the Federal troops as she fell under their power. By the end of the war, however, she was just another Southern town whose economy had failed. The blacks whose backs had supported the whole system were no longer slaves. An era had come to an end.

The ensuing years, not to put too fine a point on it, found her broke, bankrupt. During the next difficult decades, when the deterioration of her antebellum houses seemed to mock her with visions of their former splendor, she seemed upon occasion to be overtaken by a listless, almost despairing melancholy. But at the last moment, trouper that she was, she rallied. Her vast plantations had gone with the wind, certainly, yet she hung on, clung on tenaciously to her mansions without servants and her gardens without gardeners. She kept her past alive by endlessly recounting stories of her glory days to anyone who might listen; and such was the perfection of her conversational skill that they did listen.

And in the 1930's, she suddenly woke up with a start into the here and now to find that the rest of eternally forward-looking America had become fascinated—in fact obsessed—with its antebellum past. Wide awake now and eager to show herself off to the world (she always had been a show-off), she was more than willing to work on replanting her gardens and getting out the old silver and china, dusting off the chandeliers and going up to the attic where she stored most of the furniture.

Today tourism is big in Natchez. It is not, however, your common, ordinary tours that the arriving busloads of people from all over the world go on, but pilgrimages. And the people are not tourists but pilgrims. There is a Pilgrimage Garden Club and a Spring Pilgrimage and a Fall Pilgrimage, and the dedicated pilgrims pay homage to the city in increasing numbers as they view her splendidly reconstructed treasures.

Now a very grand dame, Natchez presides over what one historian has called "a veritable plantation museum unparalleled in the South." Twice a year the busloads are greeted by her natives, whom she has dressed up in hoop skirts and tossing curls. She has elderly, cheerful black men driving buggies, and she has done up expensive hotels to house her pilgrims, while her numerous shops are fairly stuffed with souvenirs, and all her restaurants serve good Southern cuisine.

Missing, of course, are those famous, spectacularly self-directed, self-willed men who led (or misled?) the American people in the early years. For a sampling of these heroes (villains?) who, at one time or another, danced to Natchez's music and enjoyed her hospitality, there were two presidents of the American people. Andrew Jackson came there in 1789 and committed himself to marrying his lady love, a divorcée. Aaron Burr, who won the same number of electoral votes as Jefferson but lost a subsequent Congressional vote, came in 1806 and committed himself to a conspiracy that he dreamed would eventually make him the Emperor of Mexico—or had he really only committed himself to colonizing a large parcel of land in Louisiana? Later Jefferson Davis, who lived in Natchez, would become President of the Confederate States and commit himself to a war.

But there are other men, not so well known, who can be seen as predecessors of our Ferriday folk.

General Claire Chennault was a military man so full of dash and derring-do that his friend Tom Corcoran suggested to Roosevelt that he envision his relationship to Chennault as that of Queen Elizabeth's to Sir Francis Drake: "Let Chennault run the show and you run him." Of his colorful military antecedents General Winfield Scott, the militia commander General John Quitman and General Ferdinand Claiborne come to mind as well as Andrew Jackson and Jefferson Davis. They were of the stuff that war heroes are made, the stuff that the South seems to produce automatically—the stuff that seemed to draw them to Natchez as to a magnet.

John F.H. Claiborne believed the proper study of history was the present, not the past. He was eyewitness to many events recorded in his historical writings. He is probably the most important source of pre-1840 Mississippi history. Stating exactly the same belief in the next century, Howard K. Smith recorded living events in his famous early news broadcasts from Berlin.

Anti-Semitism in Southern towns is a sometime thing; in

Natchez, it was a never thing. The earliest record of a Jew in Natchez was during Gayoso's time: a rich Jewish plantation owner, merchant and lumber dealer, Benjamin Monsanto, a great friend of Gayoso's, is described in one history book as "a prominent member of Natchez society. He was never persecuted for his beliefs and enjoyed the respect of his neighbors." Natchez aristocrats are said to frown on the practice of anti-Semitism as terribly "common."

The evidence of this freedom from discrimination and acceptance of the Jews is borne out in the Natchez Cemetery. There is a section of the old cemetery where the early Jews are buried. In the large Jewish section in the new part of the cemetery, Joe Pasternack, who died on August 1, 1963, is laid to rest next to his wife, Agatha, in the family plot.

One of the most interesting men in Natchez was the English planter and naturalist William Dunbar. Like Mrs. U.B. Evans after him, his real love was nature in all its forms. He was fascinated by the discovery of the exotic flora and fauna of the brave new world and by writing about these discoveries as vividly as possible. Whereas Mrs. U. B. Evans draws a cool, clear breath from an almost mystic height in her nature prose, Dunbar glories in the lush.

Soon after the Louisiana Purchase, Thomas Jefferson asked Dunbar to explore the country around Concordia Parish and send him a report on his findings.

He finds the "stately whooping crane" and the "thundering crocodile" among the fauna. But it is the vegetation around a bayou seen in the fall of the year "in the richest, most luxurious festoons" that makes his pen positively sing as he describes "a species of impenetrable curtain, variegated and spangled with all possible gradations of color from the splendid orange to the enlivening green down to the purple and blue and interspersed with bright red and russet brown."

The report sent to Jefferson did not make dull reading.

Before there was Leona Sumrall and Son and Jimmy Swaggart, there was the evangelist Lorenzo Dow, who came to Natchez in 1803. Like Leona and Son in the 1930's and Jimmy in the 1980's, he was part of a religious revival. Looking like a prophet of old, his wild hair well below his shoulders, Lorenzo was an endearing fanatic of unquestioned sincerity, as he went about preaching fiery sermons against sin and in praise of salvation. As a nice theatrical touch to drive home his Judgment Day sermons, he often paid little black boys to perch in a tree and scream or blast a horn at the precise dramatic moment.

He became a circuit preacher and had great success up and down the Natchez Trace from Mississippi to Kentucky. His immortality is fixed by two things: by the pregnant women who were so affected upon hearing his sermons that they named the male children they were bearing "Lorenzo Dow" in his honor, and by his famous definition of the predestination doctrine of Calvinism: "You're damned if you do and you're damned if you don't."

Would not Jerry Lee Lewis have been happier in Natchez's dueling times? He seems to be possessed of what can be called Natchez nerves and Natchez nerviness. There is a pattern throughout his life of acting on what he takes to be direct attacks on his personal honor. These so hurt and madden him that, without having recourse to the acceptable behavior of a duel to restore his self-esteem, he has had to descend to shooting at his foes, which include members of his band. The man who he felt personally had delivered to him the unkindest cut of all was Elvis, simply for being the King. They sent for the police when Jerry Lee turned up at the gates of Graceland with a gun.

I have said of Natchez that always in the background there is music and dancing. More and more, from the eighteenth century on, this music was being supplied by blacks. The early acknowledgment of their unique musical genius kept them in demand for performing their own songs and dances at balls, cotillions and other special celebratory occasions, making the music that the white folk danced to.

Black musical life was never limited to a single style or musical tradition, and in sophisticated, cosmopolitan Natchez, the blacks quickly absorbed white American folk songs and popular songs, along with European melodies and the marching music of the fife and drum. Hezekiah Early and his band, which features Peewee Whittaker, remains true to this tradition and draws on blues, jazz, ragtime, minstrelsy, fife and drum bands, country music, rock and roll, middle-of-the-road pop—virtually every type of secular music that has been heard in their community for the past 150 years.

It is my contention that the telluric sparks and shocks running through Natchez's soil skipped Vidalia's and plugged into the new twentieth century town of Ferriday instead.

Perhaps, though, the final word has not been said. Last year, Vidalia installed one of the largest hydroelectric plants in the world on her riverfront.

4

THE FERRIDAYS

The time has come in this chronicle to touch upon the Civil War and how Concordia Parish was affected by it and to open up, if only briefly, the Pandora's box of Reconstruction. There was no Civil War in Ferriday because Ferriday had not yet been born. In 1860, it was part of a large plantation, Helena, owned by William Ferriday and his wife Helen.

What can be said about the Civil War that has not been said by scholars who have spent their lives writing about it? Or by Civil War buffs who live in tents on former battlefields and precisely reenact the sieges? Then, too, there are white southerners who still genuinely feel the horror of that war on their own soil and feel it so strongly that it might have happened yesterday: the looting, the pillaging, the burning of houses, the civilian population treated roughly and without respect by an enemy more terrible because he was not unlike themselves.

In light of the foregoing, I have chosen instead merely to comment on two history books that hold opposing opinions, one written in the 1930's, the other fifty years later in the

1980's. The purpose is to show a shift in the point of view in journeying fifty years down the road.

Said Senator Albert Gore recently: "When a black man and a white man meet, neither knows where the other is located in the journey against prejudice. But when these men realize that each has made that journey, then there's a real bond. And that bond is stronger in the South than you'll find anywhere else in the country."

What can be said in the 1990's that was not said in the 1930's is that in Louisiana (as in the rest of the South), there are now two views to be listened to, the views of not only the whites but also the blacks.

The book *Louisiana*, edited by Bennett Wall, notes that at the close of the war, the bravest and best of young white men who fought for the Confederacy and young black men who fought for the Union were dead. In fact, of the 20,000 black men who died fighting for the Union, quite a few were Louisianans. New Orleans was captured by the Union early in the war and became a large recruiting center for blacks.

There was very little blood actually spilled in Concordia Parish. The Union troops had captured the rest of the Mississippi River towns, and Vidalia was garrisoned by black soldiers. This happened because at the beginning of the war, eighty-one percent of the plantations in Concordia Parish were owned by absentee landlords, and ninety-one percent of the population was black slaves.

Robert Dabney Calhoun, a lawyer who lived in Vidalia, wrote the only history of Concordia Parish to date, published in 1932. It is a careful study, fully documented, for the most part objective, and written in a highly felicitous style with much dry humor. When he talks of the black man's part in Reconstruction, however, his objectivity flies out the window.

Reconstruction, which began with the end of the Civil War in 1865 and went on for twelve years until the withdrawal of Federal troops in 1877 (Louisiana again under the jurisdiction of strangers!), is depicted by Calhoun as "the darkest period in the history of the state, characterized by political strife, chaos, graft and misrule. The government was in the hands of Northern carpetbaggers whose pliant tool was the negro."

In 1868, a postwar constitution for Louisiana was drawn up by ninety-eight delegates—forty-nine white and forty-nine black. *Louisiana,* published in 1984, states categorically, "The Constitution of 1868 was one of the best in the history of Louisiana. There is a strong Civil Rights clause and an integrated school system." On the other hand, in the 1930's, Calhoun was horrified by this Constitution with its provision that "All children shall be admitted to the public schools or other institutions of learning sustained by the state without distinction of race, color or other previous condition. That hideous reptile, 'social equality,' " he writes, "attempted to ride its way over the thresholds of the white public schools."

Said William Faulkner twenty years later: "To live anywhere in the world of A.D. 1955 and be against equality because of race, creed or color is to live in Alaska and be against snow."

The year 1868 was also the beginning of the Knights of the White Camellia, an organization modeled on the Ku Klux Klan, whose purpose was to intimidate blacks to keep them from voting—by murder when necessary.

As a direct result of Reconstruction in Louisiana, there came into being for the higher education of blacks Straight University, the University of New Orleans and Leland University. Eventually Straight and the University of New Orleans combined to form Dillard University. There was also an integrated university called Agricultural and Mechanical College.

One of the most significant developments of Reconstruction was the creation of independent black churches. "It is no accident that black leadership developed in these churches," writes Wall in *Louisiana,* "it was only in the church that it had a chance to do so."

Back in Concordia Parish during Reconstruction, the blacks, because of their numbers, were able to take over its government. They became sheriffs and district court clerks; served on police juries; were school board members, justices, constables and election commissioners and ran its newspaper, the *Concordia Eagle*. Writes Calhoun, horrified, "Our grand and petit juries were of a dark complexion and Old Glory was required by statute to flutter in the breeze of the temple of justice!"

In 1870, with a black population of over 9,000 and only a few hundred whites, ". . . substantial citizens [whites]," writes Calhoun, "fought fire with fire as best they could while they prayed for the dawning of the new day of white supremacy."

In 1877, with the withdrawal of Federal troops, the type of people who had been in power before the Civil War were back in power. The whites ruled supreme. All blacks were removed from official positions.

━━━

Though the Civil War never came to the town of Ferriday, it did come to a family called Ferriday, whose rising and falling fortunes were closely connected with the Helena Plantation upon whose acres that town would be built.

The Ferridays' story is in many ways a tragic one. Death stalked them. It also becomes clear, perusing courthouse records about their plantations' transactions, that they were constantly on a seesaw of buying or selling land and possessions.

The story begins with two brothers, William and Joseph Charles Ferriday, young blades born in England with property ties in the Midwest. In their twenties, they came to Natchez, the better to seek their fortunes. William married a wealthy young girl from Natchez, Helen Smith. She must have been the apple of her father's eye, because in 1827, as a wedding gift, he grandly bestowed upon her Helena Plantation which comprised 4,000 acres in Concordia Parish.

As did the majority of plantation owners in Concordia Parish, William and Helen remained in Natchez as the absentee landlords of their property across the river, a practice that continues around Vidalia to this very day.

It was in the 1830's that tragedy began to strike at the Ferridays. It would continue to do so for many, many years.

Natchez suffered repeatedly from yellow fever and cholera epidemics. As a river port, it was particularly vulnerable to contagion, and the nearby swamps were miasmic. Helen and William had fourteen children. Nine died while still in childhood. Nine times the Ferridays experienced the agony of burying a child, when in the natural course of things it would be the other way around.

Possibly to escape their sorrows, and certainly to begin afresh, on January 17, 1840, William and Helen moved their residence from Natchez to Concordia Parish. No more dilettantish absenteeism for them. They were going to be right there on the spot cultivating their plantation, attending to every detail. They were going to be planters in earnest. Helen was five months pregnant. When her baby was born, they called him Joseph Charles Ferriday after William's beloved brother. Not to confuse the two, the son went by the initials J.C. He was to be one of five children who would survive. He was to be the Ferriday whom the town is named after.

Ah, the bliss of life on a plantation. Can anything exceed it? Or, rather say, life on a well-run plantation. Take John Quitman's mouth-watering description of what it was like being a visitor at one in Natchez:

> Your coffee in the morning before sunrise, little stews and sudorifics at night and warm foot baths if you have a cold; bouquets of fresh flowers and Mint Juleps sent to your apartment; a horse and saddle at your disposal. Everything free and easy and cheerful and cordial.

Juleps often began the day. Then breakfast on the veranda. After that, hunting, riding, fishing, morning visits or chess and reading and lounging until dinner, which is served at two o'clock in great variety and most delicately cooked in the Creole style—very rich. Afterwards everybody, white and black, has disappeared. The whole household is asleep. They are enjoying the "siesta of the Italians." The ladies retire to their apartments, the gentlemen recline on the sofas, benches, hammocks, and often gypsy fashion on the grass under spreading oaks. Before sunset, the tea table is always set in the garden and there until bedtime they stroll, sing, play croquet or whist. "It is an indolent, yet charming life and one quits thinking and takes to dreaming."

Unfortunately, Helena Plantation was not able to put on a show like that. There nothing ever went smoothly. The buying and selling of assets was constant. And just five years after the Ferriday family had installed themselves, William declared bankruptcy. By 1857, they seemed to have dug themselves out of the hole and Helen had even been given, through an efficient trust officer of her father's estate, 786.80 acres in Bossier Parish in northwest Louisiana.

It is at this point, however, that the Ferridays must have taken a long hard look at themselves and decided they could not and did not want to manage the estate themselves. A solution offered itself in Archibald McDonald, bachelor, who was interested in farming the "third undivided portion" of Helena, which consisted of 3,600 acres. On July 29, 1857, a contract was drawn up between him and William "for the express purpose of carrying on the business of cotton planting." McDonald was to be the active manager, living on the plantation and receiving a yearly salary of $1,000.

In November of that same year, Helen died. Together with all their children's deaths, it was a paralyzing blow for William. What interest he had personally in the plantation now vanished. Nor had he any interest in a time-consuming partnership in overseeing that huge third undivided portion of the plantation. In fact, he wanted nothing more than to sell it quickly.

On December 28, 1857, he and McDonald went to the Concordia Parish Clerk of Court again, and this time, William expressed his desire to sell this portion of his property lock, stock and barrel for the sum of $70,000 to McDonald, the sale to take effect the very next month. For himself, he seemed to be left with hardly any of the plantation. The only thing he had exempted from sale was the house that he was to live in with his eldest daughter and her husband. The two elder sons, Robert and William Jr., had probably at this point gone up north to Pennsylvania, to

Northampton County, where they would soon make their home.

In 1865, at the end of the Civil War, William died, and his heirs, Robert, William Jr., J.C. and Emily, out of necessity, sold all the other lands that William Ferriday owned in Iowa, Illinois and Wisconsin, plus Helen's parcel in Louisiana.

By 1867, Archibald McDonald had died without heirs. William Jr. bought back the property.

By 1870, all the Ferriday heirs had agreed to sell it again.

At the last minute, however, they seem to have been saved by that same efficient trust officer for Helen's father's estate. He bought back the land for the Ferridays for around two dollars an acre. As William had sold McDonald the land for about twenty dollars an acre in 1857, it can be seen what the Civil War had done to land values in Louisiana.

Early in the 1860's, young J. C. Ferriday was sent up north to be educated (no doubt to Pennsylvania, where his two brothers could keep an eye on him). After that, he took a year off to go by steamship to the Holy Land. He was accompanied by his tutor, Mr. Cattell. Young bloods in Natchez were constantly going abroad—but not to the Holy Land. Rather, they spent their time in Europe gambling, in palaces of sin or buying prize horses for their stables. Frederick Olmsted quotes a native son on the children of Natchez planters: "You can know their children as far off as you can see them. You can tell by their walk . . . they sort of throw their legs as if they haven't got strength enough to lift them and put them down in any particular place. They do want so bad to look as if they weren't made of the same clay as the rest of God's creation." They were also prone to the flamboyant gesture. Alfred Vidal Davis, Joseph Vidal's grandson, partial to champagne, to encourage his guests to keep up with his chugalugging of the bubbly, invented a drinking glass shaped like a hunting horn; once the wine was poured, the glass could not be put down until empty.

J. C. Ferriday was of another mold. In fact, a certain earnestness can be detected in the direction of his voyage and

in his tutor's presence. It is significant that he had a tutor to
make him study and observe and that his tutor's name comes
down intact through the ages. Mr. Cattell was probably a
long-time companion of his charge, as the English-born
William Ferriday seemed to place a lot of importance on
tutors. One document drawn up just after Helen died men-
tions that their tutor "also concurred with the suggestion
that the plantation be sold."

In contrast to J. C., in the 1880's, Mark Twain would
lark about on the same trip to the Holy Land, during which
he spent much of his time comparing the state of billiard
tables in each country he visited and then writing about it
for the entertainment of his readers in *Innocents Abroad*.

After J. C. returned, he went to work for the Pennsylvania Railroad. At some point he became a lawyer. As he is not
on any of Robert Dabney Calhoun's lists of Confederate
soldiers from Concordia Parish, perhaps he stayed on in
Pennsylvania during the war. The next thing we know of
him is that he married a young lady called Emma Reeder
and, as if in a nightmare repetition of the grisly events in the
past, death struck, taking their three-year-old daughter. It
struck again and took Emma. In 1868, J. C. married again.
She was Annie Pendleton from Natchez. They had five
children, all of whom lived.

Soon after his marriage, J. C. returned to Helena Plantation with his family. It is here that J. C. at last discovered
himself. And he discovered himself not as a brilliant
planter—that never ran in the family—but as a prophet and
what must be seen as a public servant. His work with the
Pennsylvania Railroad made him aware that railroads invari-
ably made an area prosper, could even create new towns, and
that, conversely, if the railroad bypassed the area, it was
doomed.

Beginning in 1878, J. C. welcomed the railroads, offering
the right-of-way through Helena Plantation to the Natchez
and Northwestern lines, negotiating profitable terms. Neighboring plantations followed suit.

In 1887, he gave a right-of-way to the New Orleans

Northwestern and Fort Scott lines, and by that time was in a strong enough bargaining position to stipulate that the railroad had to be completed by December of 1890.

His concern was not just for the betterment of his plantation, but the betterment of Concordia Parish. He became a leader in the political, business and social life of the parish for many years. In 1888, he was elected to the powerful position of president of the police jury. His term was four years, and at the end of it, J. C. was popular enough to be elected for another four years. He never completed his second term. He died in December of 1894. His death was noted by the police jury: "At the meeting of January 5th, 1895, resolutions of regret at the death of the Honorable J. C. Ferriday were adopted."

So eager were the railroads that he was hardly cold in his grave when a quitclaim deed (a quick way of transferring ownership) was served on his widow. The plantation came into the hands of the Realty Investment Company, who laid it out as a railroad town. Why choose that site? Why did two major railroad companies, the Texas and Pacific and the Iron Mountain, choose it above all other sites in the area as a railroad depot, a terminal and a railroad roundhouse? Some telluric accounting, no doubt, was taking place.

Needing a name for the town, they called it Ferriday after the Honorable J. C., not only because it was to be on part of his property or because he invited the railroads, but also because he had made himself an integral part of the community.

THE EARLY TOWN
AND THE EVOLUTION
OF THE SMITHS

Anyone getting off a train in Ferriday in late 1903—off the
Missouri Pacific that switched in Ferriday and became the
Texas and Pacific or off robber baron Jay Gould's own darling,
the Iron Mountain—would witness that American turn-of-
the-century miracle: a town being built overnight, a town
which had no natives. The oldest things there (since it had
been woodland) were the beautiful trees: oak, cypress, magnolia, pecan, pine, chinaberry. The Realty Investment Company had simply borrowed that same cookie cutter so often
used on small towns and cut the area into blocks naming the
first, which ran up from the railroad depot, Main Street.
(Actually it was christened, but never called, Louisiana
Avenue.) The rest of the town proceeded at right angles, the
horizontal streets named after southern states, the vertical
ones, numbered.

In came the railroad workers, the real estate speculators,
the businessmen trying to guess what stores would be
needed, traveling salesmen, Mississippi (and other) gamblers
looking for new turf and people from other towns looking for

Guy Serio, town historian, in his grocery store today. (*Credit: Rhett Powell.*)

a good time. Up went the hotels, the saloons, the nightclubs, the gambling joints. In came the brothels. From the beginning, Ferriday was known as the "alcohol town." Ferriday, in fact, was not only a bad town, it was the baddest town in that whole part of the country. It was wide open. Says Guy Serio, eighty-three years old, who owns its oldest grocery store and is the acknowledged historian, "You had a lot of fights. If you went a weekend without a fight—a stabbing or a killing—you'd want to know what was wrong. If you were looking for fights, you'd get accommodated, but if you weren't looking and tending to your own business, nobody would bother you. It would begin with the gamblers and they would be tough people, but there were some people who were tough without gambling. And the sawmill people and the railroad people, they'd drink that bootleg whiskey and then go off to the women in the houses that were here downtown. Rosie Hester's were the most famous. She ran several houses. She catered more to white, but she was black and most of the fast women were black. Dr. Ratcliff had the only hospital here. There were two doctors besides him, and he lived right across from the hospital because he'd never know when they were going to call him. He always dropped in on the hospital Saturday nights just as a matter of routine. He was a good surgeon and put them back together the best he could." Later Guy Serio's wife, Grace, worked as a nurse to help sew them up. "Fights would break out in the streets and they would draw a circle of men around them watching. When Huey Long became governor in the twenties, slot machines came in. There were one-armed bandits everywhere in Ferriday—in grocery stores, gas stations and restaurants—and they stayed around a long time. With its bad name, a lot of people came into Ferriday just to tear the place up, you know? They'd fight over being drunk, over women or over something personal like their wives, things like that. Everyone had hounds for deer hunting, and if you kicked one of them fellows' hounds, you might just as well have kicked him. There was killing over hounds. It was just that tough. You don't know how tough it was."

In the end, however, respectability, coupled with optimism, triumphed. Optimism wasn't just a character trait one or two individuals might have, it informed the whole community in its earnest endeavor to succeed. "The deliberate adoption of an optimistic turn of mind," wrote William James at the turn of the century, "is the American contribution to philosophy." Of course, if you were of a caustic temperament, it could drive you crazy. It was small town optimism as much as its narrow-mindedness that provoked Sinclair Lewis's ire. In any case, in Ferriday, an optimistic respectability eventually succeeded over the jolting excitement of liquor, gambling, women—and instant mortality. What it all came down to was that Ferriday's citizens had not gone to all that trouble to build their town to let it become another Dodge City.

In came more substantial citizens, characterized as "honest, hard-working, fearless and God-fearing." They bought small farms or opened feed stores and tractor repair outfits. They opened dry goods stores, grocery stores, hardware stores, cleaning and pressing stores, barbershops, millinery stores. In came the post office and the undertaker and the florist. In came Sol Boyar's popular movie theater, showing

For law, order and business: First Rotary Club. (*Credit: The Concordia Sentinel.*)

the *Perils of Pauline* in his storefront. Up went pretty white framed houses. Up went a schoolhouse, with Miss Corinne Hutchison as its first teacher. In came Ferriday's only church service for several years, non-denominational and held at the schoolhouse every Sunday. Later came the building of Baptist and Methodist churches. Much later, in 1923, the Presbyterian Church got its start holding services in the rooms of the Sevier Hotel, whose owners were passionate Methodists.

The sidewalks were made of raised wooden planks that allowed for the Mississippi River's flooding, and the streets were unpaved. People kept hogs in the woods, identified by their brands. The cattle, too, wandered in the woods, free range, with baths every few miles so they could be dipped. Milk cows and horses wandered the streets. Austin Wilson remembers, "In the winter, the cattle would go in the woods. You'd cut the trees so the Spanish moss on them would go down to the ground. That was what the cattle ate all winter. You'd see the trees crated out and the limbs stripped off and the cattle going after the moss the minute some limb hit the ground. Cattle could hear it fall, I guess. Nature took care of a lot of things in those days."

The railroads were obliging in their desire to increase, to dominate. Within their big routes they had smaller ones that people used to go to and from the mills on hand-pumped "doodlebugs" or to go visiting their friends in other communities on day coaches. These country schedules were adjusted to the desires of the townspeople. A railroad map of the time shows the day coaches from Ferriday dropping off visitors at the tiny communities of Willits, Deer Park, Shaw and Addis, while the Louisiana and Arkansas dropped them off at Frogmore, Stacy and Wildsville.

As the town developed, so did its telluric power. There seemed to be a noteworthiness about everything that was going on there. After all, way back in the sixteenth century, when Hernando de Soto discovered the Mississippi River, had he not passed right through Ferriday and, as historians claim, been buried in what is now Ferriday's Lake St. John?

The logging companies didn't chop down just any old wood but red gum, some of the finest hardwood in the state. And the Fisher Mill, which flourished there and became one of the largest in Louisiana, was not just any old sawmill, but the one from which emerged the glamorous "Body by Fisher" for General Motors. In the early days of the automobile, a lot of wood went into the making of the bodies of cars. General Motors, as its signature of "class" rather than "mass" had even imprinted "Body by Fisher" on its wooden running boards. Its finest product was the Cadillac, the ultimate in luxury. The glossiest ads in the glossiest magazines of yesteryear are those depicting a gorgeous lady in full evening regalia, indisputably headed for the opera or the embassy, in her shiny Cadillac, with the legend beneath, "Body by Fisher."

There was a bat mill, too, whose final product was not just any old baseball bat but the renowned Louisville Slugger used by Babe Ruth and all who followed him.

There was a stave mill, too, making staves for barrels to be filled with not just any old beer but Louisiana's best, Regal Beer.

All this connected the town to the big world and gave the mill workers a sense of pride. These mills, however, had another use. In winter, the hoboes slept in them, enjoying the warmth of their boilers. Since it was a big railroad town, a lot of hoboes came in, but Ferriday was a favorite because the people were friendly, intrigued by this race of man who, as a point of honor, refused to work and whose chosen way of life was to ride the trains. "They were harmless," says Guy Serio, "they weren't the type of people to break in or anything. If they were hungry, they would ask you for food. They were pretty well educated and of course very well traveled." Says Russell Campbell, recalling his childhood, "Oh goodness, how the hoboes used to entertain me on the back steps telling stories. My mother used to feed them, take them out paper plates with food. They had some way of marking the houses where people would feed them. They told marvelous stories, wild tales and that sort of thing. We children found them enchanting. I could understand them in a way. I had the wanderlust too. But I traveled first class."

Even during hard times, when the most respectable and hard-working people were begging for any kind of job, the hoboes, with their defiance of the work ethic, were still looked upon with tolerance. There was one police chief, called "the Town Tamer," described as "really mean, even his horse was mean and would bite you," who shot a man in the back. The town managed to live with that, but when he beat up a hobo, that was too much for people and they ran him out of town.

The trains had ushered in an age of industry, and they had also ushered in an age of poetry, the importance of which would not be quite understood until decades later, when it was over. Trains took on a special mystique in popular culture as they became a vital part of the landscape. Literature used the train in many powerful ways. Tragically in *Anna Karenina*, when she kills herself by flinging herself under a train. Romantically in *Dr. Zhivago*. Wryly in Mary McCarthy's short story that shocked the forties, "The Man in the Brooks Brothers Shirt," which told a train tale of the seduction of a bright young intellectual snob of a New York girl by a wily middle-aged midwesterner; the rubbing together of two bodies and two psyches running the gamut that could only have taken place in the confines of a three-day, out-of-time, out-of-bounds cross-country journey by train.

Trains, of course, played an important part in movies.

The year that Ferriday came into being was the year that
The Great Train Robbery appeared on the screen. A train was
an excellent place to commit a robbery or, for that matter,
for the villain to tie up the heroine in cliff-hanging serials.
A train was also a good place to plan a murder, as in *Strangers
on a Train,* or to hover around while locked into a poignant,
hopeless love affair, as in *Brief Encounter.*

A great many songs were written about the legendary
Casey Jones, who heroically saved the passengers on a train
and died in the attempt.

The big bands of the forties gave us a wonderful line of
train songs like "Chatanooga Choo-Choo," and "On the
Atchison, Topeka and the Santa Fe." There was Jimmie
Rodgers, the "Singing Brakeman," whose songs were a
strange mixture of Teutonic yodeling and black blues. Later,
there was Elvis's "Mystery Train." Without trains there
would have been no blues. In a good proportion of blues
songs, the lovesick protagonists swear to outrun their sorrows
by catching a train. As Peewee Whittaker sings in "Married
Woman Blues," "I'm going to leave in the morning. I'm going
to catch that morning train. I'm going to leave you baby,
'cause I can't call your name."

According to the older generation in Ferriday, the
rhythms of the train became the very rhythms of Ferriday
itself. A train's whistle was the first thing they heard in the
morning and the last thing they heard at night, stimulating
their imagination for far-off places and giving rise to flights
of fancy. "The freight trains passing each other," says one
old-timer, "always looked to me like two buildings going in
opposite directions."

One of Ferriday's important permissions, one that is
usually sternly withheld in a small town's entrapping grip,
was the permission to *leave it.* With both the Mississippi
River beckoning at its doorstep and the trains beckoning
through it, there was never the feeling of being stifled or
smothered. People left unrepentantly and came back when
they felt like it.

As the trains had ushered in ages of industry and poetry,
they also ushered in an age of democracy, blasting away the

old feudal structure of the plantation with rolls of smoke and hoots of whistles. In came the middle class and the respectable working class.

Two young men, Howard K. Smith, Sr., and Elmer Porter, were among the earliest arrivals in the new town of Ferriday. If what we are is what we do, Elmer and Howard Sr. may be said to have exchanged identities in that swift reversal of fortune then occurring in American lives. Elmer Porter, a railroad engineer who drove the first train from Ferriday to McGehee, Arkansas, returned triumphantly and married a wealthy lady up in her "maiden" years, as they say, who purchased him a large plantation nearby called Delhi, while Howard Smith, Sr., the sixth son of a planter, became a railroad man, specifically, a train conductor. In one fell swoop, Elmer went from working class to gentry and Howard Sr. from gentry to working class.

It wasn't that simple. A train conductor could be considered beyond class, in fact, an altogether superior being. Passengers on his train understood they were in his domain and his domain only as he stood before them in his dark uniform with its smart brass buttons, his official hat with insignia, his bright silver ticket puncher and his large gold watch. Children and grown-ups alike looked up to him. He was a wise traveler who had seen it all and knew it all and never got taken in by traveling con men. In addition, Howard Sr. himself had a particularly gracious manner, a charming sociability natural to the sixth son of a planter.

Howard Sr., born around 1880, had been brought up on Lettsworth, the family plantation in the neighboring parish of Pointe Coupée. His move from planter's son to train conductor is historically noteworthy. It represented a transition downward within the plantation aristocracy, caused by the failure of the land. The Smith family tree goes back to 1640, when they came from England to Virginia. First they were military men and then they became planters. In Louisiana, they had been landowners since the late eighteenth century. However, with the great panic of 1893—the world's scariest depression until the 1930's—came the collapse of the plantation economy. Cotton was no longer King; it was a commodity nobody could afford. Yet Louisiana plantations, as did those all over the South, continued to overproduce it. Plantations, unable to scrape a living off of the land, fell into the hands of banks or corporations.

Lettsworth itself slipped away more slowly. Still, as the youngest of six, there was nothing for Howard Sr. to do there. Though his father, Dr. Ernest Smith, was both a medical man and a planter, by the turn of the century, both these incomes had vanished.

Howard Sr. was a mild-mannered, happy-go-lucky young man who didn't take life seriously. He went to college but quit before he graduated. He moved from job to job. He drifted into business—a sugar refinery. It failed. The one unusual thing he did was marry a handsome, lively young half-Cajun girl, Mamie Cates, whom he met at a dance. Though she was outside his social set, he was attracted to her good looks and vitality. She had a romantic history: her father had been a steamboat captain and both her parents had died when she was an infant. Orphaned, she and her sister were brought up by her mother's people, poor but happy backwoods Cajuns. Even in the act of marriage Howard Sr. seemed to need some outside prodding. One of Howard Sr.'s sisters was getting married, so they had a double wedding.

When Howard Sr. was hired by the Texas and Pacific line as a train conductor, the company moved him to Ferriday, which was its main terminal in northeast Louisiana. The Smiths became very much a part of the nucleus of families that made up Ferriday in its infancy. Not long before his son Howard was born in 1914 at 409 Louisiana Avenue, four or five blocks from the railroad depot, Howard Sr. even ran for mayor but got only twelve votes.

We have from Mrs. Pearl Fleming's account of baby Howard's first days a pleasant picture of a doting Mamie calling him by her pet name, Aloysius. Mrs. Fleming also notes that when the shooting started every Saturday night, Mamie popped her two children into a long box in the dining room for safety and then climbed in herself. Ferriday was certainly Howard Jr.'s first experience with trouble spots.

Add to this an early memory of his own: "The first thing I remember is a flood—water all around our house and all around the houses," as a further indication of Ferriday's dangers.

Although the Smiths left Ferriday when Howard Jr. was only three to settle down in Monroe, another railroad terminal, the importance of Ferriday in Howard Jr.'s life should not be minimized. By the time his father left Ferriday, having spent a decade and a half there, he was pretty much the man he was going to be for the rest of his life. It was in Ferriday that he firmly turned his back on his patrician past and became the sort of man unable to understand or support his son's ambitions.

Howard Sr.'s life as a train conductor, regulated but without too much responsibility, seemed ideally suited to the basic passivity of his soul. He would go on small runs, a few days there, a few days back, never going far but always in motion—perhaps there was a restlessness in him, as well, that needed to be satisfied. He was rarely at home. Psychologically, he seems to have exchanged the plain reality of domestic life for the idealized reality of the road.

"He was a typical railroad conductor," said his elder son, Prescott, eight years older than Howard Jr., "he would start up a conversation with anyone, anytime." It was ironic that Howard Sr., who could talk so easily to strangers, seemed to have nothing to say to his youngest son. Says Howard Jr., "He took me to Lettsworth once when I was about ten years old. It was after the family lost it [the house stands today, a large attractive frame house of graceful proportions amid shady trees]. There were pipes lying all around. They tried to find oil to save themselves and the place was run down, but he never told me very much about it. Somehow he didn't know what to answer to my questions. I think there was a marked absence of personality there. He just didn't make a definite impression. He was a kind man, a good man, but he was not a strong man."

It was not long before Mamie and Howard Sr. began to co-exist separately. That Mamie was a Catholic and Howard Sr. a staunch Bible-belt Baptist became a source of friction.

Through the years, with their relationship unraveling, they each seemed to knit themselves more tightly into their separate religions. Mamie insisted on raising Prescott and Howard Jr. as Catholics (she once sent Howard to parochial school but had to remove him because he couldn't understand the Italian nuns), while his father became a more ardent Baptist and even joined the Gideon Society, which distributes Bibles in hotel rooms.

Howard Jr. describes his mother as "simply an overworked housewife who got very weary of being overworked and having no money to buy proper resources." And of the marriage, "It was a bad marriage. They didn't like one another. They didn't get along."

Howard's communications with his brother were also limited. "Prescott was a rather quiet type, and he was very superior in everything, and I felt a great awe in his presence, so we rarely talked. But he didn't talk to my mother either. He was very quiet." Prescott, who eventually became a dentist, did very well in school and was outstanding in both academics and sports, winning a gold medal in track and a gold medal in debating. Could this silence at home be one of the reasons Howard Jr. became such an impassioned communicator?

Yet, at just the right place and time, Prescott extended his support to his troubled younger brother. It was the Depression and they were living in New Orleans in dire financial straits. Howard, like his brother, had won all the academic and athletic prizes in high school and was president of his class. He had gotten a scholarship to Tulane and was working in a drugstore. Says Howard, "Prescott picked me up one day and I said . . . 'I could get eighteen dollars a week if I was the boss man at this drugstore, and I could do well instead of making what I'm making now, and I could forget about college, and we'll all be better off.' And my brother," continues Howard, "who had never said a harsh word to me before, said, *'The hell you say! You wanted to be a writer! You're going to be a writer!'* And that settled it. That's the only time he ever encouraged me; I didn't know it was such a strong factor with him, but it was, so I stayed in college."

After that, Howard Smith, born of Ferriday, gave himself permission to leave. Like his father, he would become a traveling man.

At Tulane, Howard worked hard. He graduated Phi Beta Kappa, president of the student body and a track star. He aimed to win a Rhodes scholarship that would take him to Oxford, but it turned out he was one academic credit short. In 1936, as has been described, he went to Germany to get this extra credit at the University of Heidelberg. Why Germany? "I am a historian. A current historian," Howard said later. Germany, he realized, was the trouble spot of Europe. It was where current history was being made. What he saw in Nazi Germany confirmed his instinct that there was going to be a world war.

At the end of his course, he returned to New Orleans and worked briefly on a newspaper. When he learned that he had won the Rhodes scholarship, he went back to Germany for another intense exploration before turning up at Oxford in the fall of 1937.

Oxford was heady stuff for the young Louisiana scholar. But he found his balance almost immediately. During his two-year stay, he became the first American student to become president of its Labour Club of 1,000 members. How did he pull this off? Handsome, lanky, engaging, with the air of a willing leader, he clearly knew how to run things. But he also had something special the rest of the students didn't have: firsthand, up-to-date knowledge of Germany. Howard was the expert. The Labour Club at the time was violently opposed to the Tories' disgraceful appeasement of Hitler. At least once a week, Howard made the rounds of the colleges to lecture about Germany and its imminent threat to England. He wrote a weekly column in the club's newspaper. In the wee hours of the morning, he sneaked out with other schoolmates, painting political slogans like "Chamberlain must go!" and "Throw out the men of Munich!" around town. He picketed the Prime Minister's residence, wearing a sandwich board with incendiary slogans. He marched on Trafalgar Square. At the end of a term, he rushed back to Germany "to sharpen my zeal."

Of these experiences he has written, "I drank deep of the political spring and had more fun than I have had before or since."

There is something called Oxford flamboyance indigenous to the turf: its attitude is cool, scholarly, sweeping and well versed in shock tactics. Most American Rhodes scholars disregard it as irrelevant; Howard embraced it. Oxford's influence on him was deep and enduring.

He left Oxford and worked for the United Press in London and Copenhagen. The year 1941 found him in Berlin, where he had become the news broadcaster for CBS. His experiences formed the basis for his first book *The Last Train from Berlin*. In a good first book, the sound of a new author's voice is plainly heard. Howard's voice is loud and clear: young, exuberant, disarmingly cocky, rich in scorn and contempt for the Nazi regime. About Hitler he says:

"It is only by the most fantastic combination and concourse of circumstances imaginable that a second-rate psychopath housepainter with a third-rate intellect could become the head of a nation in which he is a rank foreigner."

The book is also a brilliant piece of investigative reporting. He is especially good as he leads the reader step by step, clue by clue, behind the impenetrable wall of propaganda erected by the Nazis to hide from their people their disastrous defeat in Russia—the defeat that broke their war machine.

The Nazi authorities began monitoring his broadcasts. A petty nuisance campaign was carried on against him. He was given a typewriter with one key missing. The intervals in which he was not banned from the air for some misdemeanor became shorter. His scripts were slaughtered. He was kicked off the air. He escaped on the last train out of Berlin under cliff-hanging circumstances.

His book, written in six weeks when he was twenty-seven, became a best-seller.

When Howard stepped off the train in Switzerland, he was met by Benedicte Traberg, a striking young Danish girl, a war correspondent whom he met in Berlin. They married and have not been separated since.

In 1942, when America entered the war, they journeyed to France covering the story of its Underground and then to Holland, Howard writing articles for the *New York Times* and *Life*. In 1945, he covered Russia's part in the surrender of Germany and the Nuremberg trials.

He returned to London, having been appointed by Ed Murrow to become CBS's chief European correspondent and director of the London bureau, a post he maintained for eleven years. The year 1957 found him in Washington as CBS's chief correspondent and manager of its bureau there. In 1962, he switched to ABC, where he remained for seventeen years. Nowadays, he lectures around the country to business groups and accepts selected television assignments.

Says Benedicte, "We spend one-third of our time on the road." The phrase is theatrical and his concerns have often been theatrical, another Ferriday trait. He has been in sixteen movies playing himself and is proud that he is the only anchorman to have a Screen Actors Guild card.

Howard has won every important award given for excellence in broadcasting, including the Peabody Award, the Emmy, the Du Pont Commentary Award, the Lowell Thomas Award, the Overseas Press Club Award six times and a Friars Club "Oscar" (given to three outstanding American broadcast journalists, the others being Walter Cronkite and David Brinkley).

He has received eighteen honorary doctorate degrees from American universities.

He moderated the first presidential debate on television between Kennedy and Nixon in 1960, and the debate between Carter and Reagan in 1980. He has monitored elections in Central America.

With all the honors accrued, it looks as if it has been pretty smooth sailing for Howard. But beneath the concord there has always been discord. And beneath the scholarly manner, the Oxford flamboyance remains. Howard longed for the freedom given to the political newspaper columnist to say what he felt, but would never, it seems, give up the shock value of saying it live on TV. "He clashes repeatedly with

Howard K. Smith, anchorman and pundit, around the time he moderated the first televised Kennedy/Nixon debate, 1960. *(Credit: Howard K. Smith private collection.)*

network management on questions of editorializing and commentary," a colleague said back in 1960.

To Howard it was an old story:

In 1941, the BBC refused to let him broadcast in London because he would not alter his criticism of American and British policy in his script.

In 1949, in his book *The State of Europe,* he stirred things up by advocating welfare states for the free European countries. He also pointed out that, since the satellite countries had never had democracy, they were much better off under the Communists than under their pre-war tyrannical dictators. This earned him a place in *Red Channels,* a blacklisting publication.

During the Suez Crisis in 1956, over which England

and Egypt almost came to war, he had the novel idea of doing a program from the Egyptian point of view.

In 1960, CBS dropped Howard for a night because he refused to alter his script pointing out the differences between Eisenhower's foreign policy and Nixon's.

Soon after, when Kennedy became President, Howard attacked his domestic policy, which again led to disputes. Not too long after, he resigned or was fired from CBS. It was said that anyone but Howard would have been fired long ago, but that he was "just so good they couldn't let him go." He was known as the intellectual dean of CBS.

Howard went to ABC. In 1962, when Nixon, after being defeated in his race for governor of California stated he would retire, Howard presented a broadcast called "The Political Obituary of Richard M. Nixon." The program produced a blizzard of protest for putting on the air Alger Hiss, a convicted perjurer first accused by Richard Nixon for Communist activities. There were pickets and bomb threats, and Howard was accused both of being a pinko and of trying to get his ratings up. ABC stood by him. Howard was the first newscaster to conduct a one-on-one interview with Nixon and the first to demand his resignation over Watergate.

Another program of his called "Is Baseball a Bore?" had Howard stating that the game was nine-tenths inaction and one-tenth action.

Up to 1966, Howard could be labeled an argumentative progressive. That year, he went to Vietnam to film reports for ABC. To everybody's astonishment he swung around politically one-hundred-eighty degrees and came back fiercely hawkish. In an editorial in the right-wing *National Review* in 1967, he condemned *New York Times* anti-war editorials and accused its foreign correspondents of "purveying Communist propaganda" with their pessimistic and defeatist stories. He advocated escalation of the war and total destruction of North Vietnam, plus the invasion of Laos and Cambodia. Later, he gave an interesting explanation for his stand: "I *hated* that war," he said. "I just felt something had to be done there. My ideas were shaped by Adolf Hitler, by what I saw in Germany."

Domestically, Howard's life has run smoothly. Interestingly, Benedicte says, "When I married Howard, it was as if I married an orphan." Their marriage has been a happy one. Their home life is very different from that of Howard's separately co-existing parents. They are close—so close it is impossible to know where one leaves off and the other begins. Benedicte is not only his wife, but his manager, his agent and his social secretary as well. She is a forcefully managing woman, and he seems delighted to be thus managed. Instead of making order out of chaos, she makes still more order out of order, and every moment of their lives is timed down to the split second. When they travel, they stay on Washington time and eat and sleep accordingly. Into their close circle are woven their children, Jack and Catherine. Howard emphasizes this closeness with such indicative remarks as, "We have a saying in our family for crises, 'Cheer up, it might be worse. Hitler might have won the war.'"

Whether they are living in a Regency house in London or on the Potomac or, as now, in Bethesda, their houses are filled with antique treasures. One writer referred to a home of theirs as "baronial." Perhaps more accurately, they could all be called antebellum.

In September 1989, Ted Koppel, on a "Nightline" program about World War II, included three of that era's most distinguished newscasters, Eric Sevareid, Robert Trout and Howard K. Smith. Everything these giants had to say was fascinating, but it was interesting that it was to Howard that Koppel would turn to every so often saying, "Howard, put us right about that" or "Sum it up for us, will you Howard?"

But what of Elmer Porter, the former train engineer and newly made plantation owner, back in those early days of Ferriday? Was Howard's father envious of him? Probably not; submerged in his own world, he was sufficient unto it. Was Elmer envious of Howard Sr. and his romance with the railroad? Very probably—all the crops at Delhi plantation were ruined that first year. He didn't give up; he sent for his relatives, farmers up in Illinois, but even so, it was quite a while before they got the hang of delta soil. And many times during this difficult period, one can be sure, he would have given anything to be back in the exhilarating freedom of an engineer's seat.

GENERAL CLAIRE LEE CHENNAULT

Lake St. John, a few miles from Ferriday's city limits, is a beauty spot toward which, from earliest times, Ferridians gravitated, building summer or year-round homes. Many plantations bordered it, and it has inspired a variety of domestic architecture on its shores. It is a long, narrow lake shaped like a lazy horseshoe. Driving around, you see the kind of picturesque scene that encourages you to send your astral self into each house, bungalow, cottage and camp, urges you to drop everything, buy a place there and sit all day watching the sun dancing on the water, staring at the lake's changing colors from brown to black, from gold to silver, savoring the freshness of it in the morning and the philosophical peace of it at twilight.

That peace was broken from the 1920's to the 1950's by the bewitching music-on-water sound of a dance band pulsating across it, emanating from the dance pavillion at Coola Cusa.

Its peace was further attacked in the 1930's by the barnstorming aviator Captain Claire Lee Chennault.

General Claire Lee Chennault. (*Credit: State Archives, Baton Rouge.*)

They would say of him during World War II that he was "the one genius that the war on the Asiatic mainland has yet produced." They would also say of him and the fighter pilots under his command, who called themselves the Flying Tigers, that they wrote "a never-to-be-forgotten record across the skies of Asia, and are now a part of American glory." Further, they would say "the rest of the world held its breath and marveled at the shining story of venture and vision of a few American volunteers winning victory after victory."

To top it all, in 1942, when the war news was bad all over the world, Chennault's Flying Tigers so triumphed over the Japanese air force that they unleashed some fine Churchillian prose:

The magnificent victory these Americans won in the air over the paddy fields of Burma are comparable in character, if not in scope, with those won by the Royal Air Force over the orchards and hop fields of Kent in the Battle of Britain.

He had coal black hair and coal black eyes. He had stern, handsome features marred by a leathery skin as lined and scarred as aged bark. In profile, he had a chin so stubborn that it threatened to meet his nose, but full face, he looked very like John Wayne at his most heroic. He chain-smoked Camel cigarettes and had chronic bronchitis that was always accompanied by a high fever. For the latter half of his life he was stone deaf.

In England, they were told he was an American Indian. In China, some of his men were certain he was part Chinese, around his eyes anyway, which sat flat on his face. Actually, Chennault, born in 1893, gloried in his warrior ancestry and recited it often. The first Chennault came to America from Alsace-Lorraine and fought with Lafayette in the American Revolution. In the course of this Chennault's Western migration, his line crossed with that of Sam Houston, fighter and founder of Texas, and the Confederate general Robert E. Lee. Claire Lee's father was named Stonewall after Stonewall Jackson. Heroes have heroes.

If Howard K. Smith's first memory was that of a town with water around houses, Claire Lee Chennault's earliest recollections were, he has written, of "roaming the oak woods and moss-draped cypress swamps of the Mississippi flood plains in northeast Louisiana." Hunting in the woods became a passion that never left him, and as for fishing, he was to say, "I have fished all over the world, but a spring never passes without my thoughts turning to bass on the Tensas River" (which forms the boundary between Tensas Parish and Concordia Parish).

What Chennault shared with the other prominent people who were born or made their homes in this tiny dot in northeast Louisiana was the vigorous use he made of his environment; he used his surroundings for all they were worth.

Chennault didn't just appreciate the beauty of wild nature that surrounded him on the edge of his father's cotton farm, he loved it with a mystical ardor. To hunt game, to kill his prey and bring it back home to the dinner table, thrilled him. Later on, the connection between stalking and shooting his prey in the air and teaching his pilots to fight enemy planes became obvious. "It's hard," he once remarked, "to teach a fighter pilot how to shoot who hasn't bagged a duck on the wing." A killer instinct to outwit the enemy was conceived in these woods.

As a child, Chennault would spend as long as a week at a time in these woods. He would ask no playmates to join him. Alone with his gun he would make camp, eat berries and kill game for food. He would also take great risks, for the woods then were not only full of wild turkey and deer but wolves and bears. In short, he was one of those youths who keep putting themselves in desperate situations in order to feel fully alive, where most others would feel half-dead with fright. Young Chennault felt most at ease when buried deep in the woods.

When he was five, his mother died, leaving his father inconsolable. The young boy took to the woods.

He went to school in Gilbert, a town some twenty-five miles from where he would eventually make his home on Ferriday's Lake St. John.

So often people who go on to distinguish themselves have, in their pasts, a gifted grade-school teacher who sees potential and encourages them. Such a one was Lottie Barnes to Claire Lee Chennault.

Lottie saw in Chennault a pupil who excelled in everything—except popularity. She not only saw his potential, she saw his loneliness, too. She went out of her way to take walks and horseback rides with him. She was sympathetic to his passion for the woods and rivers, but she also encouraged him to be ambitious scholastically, hoping it might divert him from his almost fanatic competitiveness. He had to be the best hunter, the best fisher, the best athlete among his schoolmates. It wasn't a trait that endeared him to his peers. He read omnivorously about war and took to quoting sources, which, in his case, were Scipio Africanus, Hannibal and Stonewall Jackson.

Interestingly, a while after the boy had formed this bond

with her, Lottie married his father. Chennault seems to have sublimated any Oedipal anguish and gone on worshiping her, learning from her and basking in her approval. Later, he would go on to emulating her. He, too, would become a teacher.

Whatever his achievements to come—his courage, his bravery, his unequaled brilliance as a master strategist—all these qualities might have counted for nothing if he had not been something else as well: an inspired teacher.

After Lottie married his father, she was still, Chennault has written, "my best and almost only companion." She died suddenly five years later, when he was fifteen. "I was alone again and never found another companion whom I could so completely admire, respect and love."

It is hard to lose your mother twice.

After her death, he hardened into an outsider. His inability to get along with boys his own age or older got worse. It would be a problem all his life. He would put people off by doing things too quickly, too well and too confidently. But Chennault was also a *gregarious* outsider. When a front door slammed shut in his face, he hastened to slip in through the back door.

There was a chink in his armor. Though he was never popular with the older boys whose leadership he refused to follow, instead of fighting his battles alone, he organized younger boys, who accepted his leadership. This was as true of him as an adolescent as it was when, at the age of fifty-one, he turned a handful of raw young pilots into incomparable fighters, while himself fighting constantly with his superiors.

He kept skipping grades, so he was only fifteen when he went to Louisiana State University. There the older boys didn't like him any better than they had back home. His college career was notable chiefly for his getting himself expelled every spring term so that he could go back home and fish. They accepted him back every autumn because his grades were good.

Finally, he quit LSU and went to the state teachers' college. This was much more to his liking. The job that was the most fun for him was teaching in a one-room school-house in Athens, Louisiana. No teacher had ever stayed more than a term there because the rough, oversized farm boys were such terrors. He took them on, one by one, and after they bit the dust, he had no trouble at all.

In 1911, he married his first wife, Nell Thompson from Waterproof. Soon they had two children. This made their economic problems acute. Chennault drifted through the South from school to school, always in search of higher pay. He now had a woman he loved and children of his own to teach.

But always there was something else he yearned for, some bright new world that hadn't already been conquered.

In 1910, he saw his first plane, a rickety biplane wobbling through the air at the Louisiana State Fair, and for the first time, his ambitions flew upward.

When America went into World War I in 1917, he signed up immediately and went to Officer's Training School, emerging as a first lieutenant. The war was over before he was shipped out.

He applied for flight training but was turned down. A twenty-six-year-old father of three children is not a good candidate to be a pilot. Cleverly, he got himself assigned to army air bases and talked friendly instructors into taking him up. Chennault was turned down three times before he was accepted to flight training school. By then he was a veteran flyer. He almost washed out due to a difference of opinion with an instructor on how to operate a plane. Chennault, it would seem, was congenitally incapable of following orders with which he disagreed.

He was able to talk his way back in and was taken over by a first-rate teacher, Ernie Allison, who gave him his first taste of acrobatics. Chennault thrilled to the feeling of at last merging himself with the machine into a single instrument. He was, he has said, "hooked forever like a bass on the Tensas River." He became one of the best stunt flyers in the country.

In Texas in 1928, he worked on the new concept of the *paratrooper*, perfecting it so that the paratroopers landed on the ground at the same time as the machine guns attached to parachutes did. Less than a minute after they landed, the troopers were able to open fire. The army brass's reaction was sharp: "Stop that parachute nonsense before someone is hurt."

In 1930, Chennault was a student at a tactical school in Virginia. His instructors, several World War I aces, were still teaching the tactics of the Dawn Patrol, the one-on-one dogfighters of World War I. Chennault felt this was all wrong. The dogfight looked to him as dated as knights in armor jousting. Ever since his acrobatic days, Chennault had been working on problems of aerial combat. There is one way to get along in the army: keep your mouth shut and agree with your superiors. Impulsively, he sent off an eight-page treatise to the higher-ups violently disagreeing with everything being taught and enumerating his reasons. It got in the hands of a general who passed it on with an angry, "Who is this damned fellow, Chennault?" Chennault, he was told, was a constant thorn in their side with his crackpot theories.

He was sent to Maxwell Field, Alabama, to be an instructor. The reasoning went that if a troublemaker were made to teach, he would have to teach what he was told to. Instead, the colonel in charge was fascinated by Chennault's theories and urged him to put them into practice with the cadet pilots.

Chennault's theories were to revolutionize aerial warfare. They centered around the importance of using small, flexible fighter airplanes sent up in teams of two or three, perfectly coordinated. These would be used to attack a single enemy plane. The advantages were tremendous, as the firepower of two planes against one is not merely two-to-one but four-to-one; similarly, three planes against one have the firepower of nine-to-one. He wrote a book called *The Role of Defensive Pursuit,* which received no attention at the time, but has since become a textbook.

He worked with his best cadets on an acrobatic formation which came to be known as the Three Men on a Flying Trapeze. They performed in air shows all over the country, and often they performed over Lake St. John, flying over his home. As always, making full use of his environment, he used Lake St. John itself for target practice, sending up three pilots to shoot targets set up in the lake, firing in precision. As there were no radios in the P-12s they were flying, hand signals had to be used.

In 1936, he collapsed with severe bronchitis, exhaustion and, probably, frustration. Army doctors had pronounced him half-deaf, and as they were about to retire him, he quit. He returned to his home on Lake St. John and began to think seriously of becoming a farmer.

He received a letter from Madame Chiang Kai-shek, Secretary of the Chinese air force. Following up General Mow's reports on Chennault from a Miami air show, she invited him to come to China for three months to inspect its air force. China was at war with Japan. Chennault could not resist.

———

In Howard K. Smith's war there were names like Paris, Brussels, Berlin and London. In Chennault's war there were names like Singapore, Rangoon, Mandalay and Kunming.

In 1937, Chennault arrived in China to find it an international bouillabaisse of nationalities. China was at war with Japan. Italians were training Chinese pilots. Germans were training Chinese troops. Russians sent ground crews, planes and first-rate pilots. And withal China was close to defeat.

Soon Chennault met his boss, Madame Chiang. Dazzled by her beauty, her manner and her dulcet tones from the American South where she was raised, he fell for her from a great height. "She will always be a Princess to me," he wrote rapturously in his diary. He met the tempermental Generalissimo Chiang and was delighted to find that they agreed over the importance of aerial defense.

Chennault was given a free hand to build up China's air power. It was a vast undertaking. The Chinese pilots had been badly trained, China's air fleet was almost nonexistent and even the airfields' runways were without proper surfacing, making it dangerous to take off or land.

What he did so magnificently was an exercise in pure communication. He started a network of ground air-raid warnings that ran 750 miles through southern China, which would become the most efficient warning system yet invented. He developed it to such a degree that by the time the enemy was within range, fighter pilots would already know the number of Japanese planes, their type, their altitude and where they were headed.

Chennault himself, in his own plane, fought the Japanese. It is recorded that he downed forty of their planes. He fought side by side with the Russians and with an assortment of mercenaries who were Dutch, French and American.

These mercenaries, when they were not flying, were carousing at night with Chinese and Russian girls. Chennault underwent a sea change: the devoted family man (he now had eight children) became a ladies' man, attracted to and attracting these girls. He became particularly fond of Oriental women and was close friends with a number of them.

But Chennault was enamored of all China. It was his dream come true, just when he had despaired. Here was a rescuing action he could perform that would save a whole nation.

On October 8, 1937, the United States and Britain condemned Japan's aggression and stopped supplying the Japanese with war goods. Chennault was no politician, but he was sure by then that the Japanese, bolstered by their success in China, would soon take over strategic Burma and then attack America.

Chennault's contract with the Chiangs was for only three months. When the time was up, he pledged himself to them for the rest of the war. It was a honeymoon that would never end. They would forever have his loyalty and fealty. Chennault would say of Chiang that he considered him "one of the two or three greatest military and political leaders of the time."

To his home on Lake St. John he wrote Nell to send his favorite shotgun. To keep his equilibrium over the grave situation in China, he went duck shooting, but at the same time he wrote in his diary, "Too much trouble to record a diary of continued trouble."

Chennault studied the Japanese planes and their pilots exhaustively. After a while, to the amazement of spectators, he could describe each detailed move that a Japanese squadron would make before it actually made it. With maps and stratagems, he was able to state to the Chiangs categorically that, given a hundred planes and a hundred trained pilots from America, he could rid China's mainland of the Japanese in six months.

They took him seriously and sent him to America.

In the fall of 1940, Chennault appeared in Washington. The climate was isolationist; the concern only for the war in Europe. Chennault needed a miracle to get what he wanted. A powerful friend of China was Thomas Corcoran, confidante of Roosevelt. Chennault met with him and began putting forth his proposals. At first, Corcoran wondered if this man were not mad; ten minutes later he wrote him off as a fanatic; then he began listening and learning from this born teacher. Corcoran urged Roosevelt to listen to him, too. The upshot of the matter was that Roosevelt gave his consent—"unofficially official"—to a hundred planes and a hundred volunteers for China.

Chennault went around the country recruiting at air bases for army, navy and marine flyers, as well as support personnel. He asked them to join for love of adventure and hope of gain. Their salaries ranged from $250 a month to $750. The pilots would be getting $600 a month and, just as invitingly, $500 for every Japanese plane destroyed. But he also appealed to their patriotism, convincing them that war between America and Japan was imminent. Pearl Harbor was only nine months away.

─────

When the American Volunteer Group, as it was called, disembarked in Rangoon, Chennault was there to meet them. There were only sixty-eight P-40s and seventy pilots.

Chennault stood at the dock looking adventurous and exuding informality.

Before they left for the Toungoo airfield, this unruly, rowdy, highly individualistic group went out on the town. Some got drunk and ripped the sarongs off Burmese ladies and others got kicked out of religious pagodas for wearing their cowboy boots. Many of them would fly in cowboy boots.

At Toungoo, Chennault began training the soon-to-be-called Flying Tigers. The born teacher quickly won their respect and attention. He told them to forget everything they had ever learned about dogfights, that they would always work in teams and always fight in pairs, like "the two hands of a boxer in a ring," the lead plane to go in for the kill, and the wing man to protect him. He taught them where the strengths and weaknesses of both the American P-40s and Japanese Zeros lay and how to use both to their advantage.
Up in the air or down on the ground he seemed never to leave their sides. He worked with them and then he played baseball with them.

Days after America declared war on Japan in December of 1941, Chennault unleashed his Flying Tigers in their P-40s against the Japanese Zeros. They performed gloriously. He had drawn from his men their full capacity for heroism, their ability to face death daily, high-heartedly and gallantly and in perfect harmony with the patriotic demands of the time.

The spectacular victories of a handful of obscure "American Soldiers of Fortune and their Colonel Chennault" burst upon the front pages of the newspapers and were featured in the newsreels; Chennault became a household word, as did the Flying Tigers.

Chennault was in his element fighting just the sort of war he fought best: loosely organized, desperate, personal and improvised. His ingenuity was astounding. He kept the Chinese building airfields everywhere—sometimes behind enemy lines—so that the Tigers could confuse the Japanese by never landing at the same airfield from which they had taken off. Next to each airfield, the Chinese built a dummy airfield with dummy airplanes made out of painted canvas stuffed with hay. The Japanese would bomb these false targets, and the hay caught fire convincingly. The men had painted their P-40s' snouts with big tiger shark teeth "to scare the superstitious Japanese" (hence the name Flying Tigers). Often their planes would be repainted and new numbers put on them. The Japanese always thought there were at least 200 planes and as many pilots.

The American Volunteer Group developed into the China Air Task Force and went on to become the Fourteenth Air Force. But always they were the smallest arm of the air force and the most elite. Chennault himself progressed from a colonel in the Chinese army to a brigadier general in the U.S. Air Force and then to major general. He was decorated by every Allied country. *Time, Life* and *Look* magazines did cover stories on him.

Such celebrity could not fail to spark feelings of resentment from other branches of the service stationed in the China-Burma-India theater.

Soon another war was going on that would often seem to take precedence over the one with Japan. It was the war of the generals—General Joseph W. Stilwell and General Chennault. They differed with every fiber of their bodies over the most important decision they would ever be concerned with: how to beat the Japanese. "Vinegar Joe" Stilwell, commanding general of the CBI theater, was an infantry man and was sure the only way to win the war was on foot. General Chennault knew it was going to be won in the air. Their differences were irreconcilable. Neither would ever see the other's way of thinking. General Stilwell was Chennault's superior. Unfortunately, he was also in charge of the distribution of supplies. The battle they fought came to be known as the Battle of the Hump, the Hump being the route over the Himalayas which was the Flying Tigers' only supply line now that the Burma Road had fallen to the enemy.

Odd things were happening to their supplies.

In the middle of the war, Colonel Robert Lee Scott first flew supplies over the Hump to Kunming, where the Flying Tigers were based. Arriving, he was surprised to find that the Flying Tigers he met were hostile and surly (though he noticed when they lit cigarettes he offered them that their hands shook). Scott couldn't figure out why he wasn't being treated like Santa Claus. They told him to unpack the supplies. He was shocked to find that instead of the needed aviation gasoline, machine gun ammunition, bombs, or even cigarettes and whiskey, there was instead a large consignment of Chinese paper money (worthless to them), some embossed stationery, metal cabinets, coil after coil of woven hemp rope and a heavy safe. The next time he flew from India with his load, Scott and his crew had ascertained in mid-air what was in it, dumped it all overboard, went back and reloaded with the commodities that were needed. After this, several other pilots in the know did the same. Once, when they were expecting overdue mail from the states, a mysterious consignment of tennis shoes was flown in marked for the Chinese army.

Chennault was not the only commander Stilwell couldn't get along with. He couldn't get along with Generalissimo Chiang either, whom he called "the Peanut." In front of a large Allied conference, Stilwell was asked what he thought of Chiang. "He is a vacillating, tricky, undependable old scoundrel who never keeps his word," he answered. Asked the same question, Chennault replied: "He has never broken a promise or a commitment to me."

Roosevelt wrote to General George Marshall that his friend Stilwell had "exactly the wrong approach in dealing with General Chiang, who, after all, can not be expected as a Chinese to use the same methods that we do. When Stilwell speaks of talking to him in sterner tones, he goes about it just the wrong way."

"Chiang," Roosevelt goes on to say, "came up the hard way to rule 400 million people as chief executive and as commander-in-chief. One cannot speak sternly to a man like that or extract commitments from him as we might do from the Sultan of Morocco."

Meanwhile, the war of the generals accelerated. Stilwell found Chennault insubordinate, blind to the big picture and only interested in seeing his own theories work out. In a letter to President Roosevelt, Chennault had this to say of

Stilwell as strategist: "The present plan of defense . . . is that of the standard, orthodox, rigid military mind. It has no military value. It shows a complete lack of conception of the true use of air power or even basic military strategy."

The battle got hotter. Chennault wired Stilwell for emergency supplies against a new Japanese build-up. Stilwell replied he was unable to do anything until "the emergency is unmistakable."

With another exchange of wires over Stilwell's order that Chennault's pilots defend Ch'eng-tu, one can fairly hear Chennault's dismissive contempt in "the defense of the Ch'eng-tu area is child's play compared to the more difficult problems that confront us," matched by the controlled fury of Stilwell's "I am glad to hear the defense of Ch'eng-tu is child's play . . . it is a relief to know you have no problems at Ch'eng-tu."

For whatever reason, the Flying Tigers, now the Fourteenth Air Force, were often grounded for lack of supplies.

They didn't think it was funny. Said one Flying Tiger, "The bitterness of those who flew for Chennault lasted a long time. They saw that human jealousies and ignorance killed their own friends and, worse, rendered their own sacrifices useless."

Things began happening fast. Stilwell continued to treat Chiang like the Sultan of Morocco. Chiang threw one of his famous tantrums and became intransigent. In the fall of 1944, Stilwell was recalled. General Albert Wedemeyer took his place and Sino-American relations were re-established. Wedemeyer and Chennault worked smoothly together, as did General Curtis LeMay and his contingent of bombers. Transporting the Flying Tigers' supplies over the Hump became top priority. In December 1944, their assault on the enemy began. Wave after wave of bombarding planes, in unison with Chennault's flyers, blasted the air. On May 15, 1944, there was an eerie silence. The Japanese air force in China was annihilated. As Chennault predicted, it had taken six months.

But army politics and loyalties were grinding exceeding fine. General Stilwell had many friends in high places, such

Claire Lee Chennault commemorated in a U.S. Postage stamp, September 1990, and as a statue erected by the people of the Republic of China, 1976, in Baton Rouge.

as General George Marshall and General Henry "Hap" Arnold. General Chennault was summarily removed from his scene of triumph. He was to be transferred elsewhere as a wing commander. Instead, he resigned.

The Chinese, however, did not deprive him of his triumph. Huge crowds turned out to pay homage to their savior in every city on his farewell tour. His commitment to the Chiangs and Nationalist China was total.

Chennault and Nell were divorced. He married Anna Chen, a beautiful, intelligent, young Chinese journalist who bore him two children, bringing the number of his children to ten.

But there was no peace for the general—or, rather, Chennault found his peace in war.

In the last phase of his life, he formed his own airline, the Civil Air Transport. Not a shot was fired by his pilots. Their purpose was to airlift food and supplies and troops to help Chiang's forces against the Communists. Later it was used in covert operations by the CIA.

He was to die of cancer at the age of sixty-five, achieving the rank of lieutenant general. He was buried with full military honors at Arlington National Cemetery. Since then, there has been a statue erected in his honor in Baton Rouge by the people of the Republic of China in 1976. And in September of 1990, he was commemorated on a 40-cent U.S. postage stamp.

Before his death, there was one last deer hunting season back home by the Tensas River with his old friend Tom Corcoran. Deer went by but Chennault didn't shoot. "I've reached the point," he told Corcoran, "where I would rather see them alive and beautiful than just a hunk of meat . . . Let's go and get some fish. I don't feel the same way about fish."

The Flying Tigers' spirit lives on. At Tianan-men Square in Beijing during the student uprising in 1989, eleven leaders of a motorbike group served as messengers during the demonstrations. They called themselves the Flying Tigers.

THE PASTERNACKS

On October 16, 1950, Hollywood's Joe Pasternak wrote on MGM stationery to Ferriday's Joe Pasternack, saluting him as follows: "Dear Mr. Pasternack—or should I say—Dear Friend—or Dear Relative—or Dear Countryman?" Then follows his request: It seems that his friend George Sidney, while in Natchez shooting *Show Boat* with Ava Gardner and Howard Keel, had recently met Ferriday Joe, who had told Sidney that he was Hungarian. If this were true, said Hollywood Joe, he would certainly like to know all about him and where he came from and perhaps they will discover they are long lost cousins! He added in a jocular Hungarian vein, "I am not in the market for anything." And then seriously again, "I just want to find out these things."

Who were these people anyway?

Hollywood Joe Pasternak was a successful producer who had left his home in Szilagy-Somlyo, Hungary, in his teens to go to America. He produced hit musicals for the screen and helped popularize classical music in them. He is credited with having saved Universal Studios from financial disaster

with a string of Deanna Durbin films. He is also credited
with saving the career of Marlene Dietrich by casting her
rough and ready in *Destry Rides Again*. He made Mario Lanza
a star by casting him in *The Great Caruso*.

George Sidney was a top MGM director of such smash
musicals as *Annie Get Your Gun, Show Boat, Bye, Bye Birdie,
Kiss Me Kate* and *Pal Joey*.

And Ferriday Joe Pasternack was the owner of one of the
best known stores in northeast Louisiana.

If, however, you had asked about each of them several
decades before, you would have been asking about a busboy,
a messenger and a sweeper of a store.

Hollywood Joe Pasternak had begun as a busboy at Paramount Studios. Shortly thereafter, he became a second
assistant director. Three short years later, he was the manager of Universal Studios' operations in Berlin. By 1935, he
was back in America producing his successful musicals.

George Sidney, born on Long Island, began his Hollywood
career as a messenger boy. The following year, he was a film
editor, then, barely twenty years old, he was directing MGM
screen tests. Soon he was directing MGM feature films.

If these two success stories seem like something out of a
Hollywood film fantasy, they were. Art was simply imitating
life.

The American way of success at this time dictated that
you succeed not by studying but by *doing*. No doubt the
reason for their swift ascents was that almost all the powers
at the studios had begun the same way.

In Ferriday Joe's case, the store whose floors he was
sweeping happened to be his father's. Nevertheless, he was
agreeable to the task. It was what was expected of him as a
youngster; it was what his son Joe Jr. would also do in turn.

According to Joe Jr. (or in southern nomenclature Little
Joe as opposed to his father, Big Joe), the two Pasternacks did
get together (Hollywood Joe was in New Orleans producing
The Belle of New Orleans). They enjoyed each other's company and decided that, yes, probably they were related.

If Hollywood Joe's Horatio Alger story is an American

story, his search for his roots is an American Jewish one. Ferriday Joe's story is yet another and perhaps the most interesting of all, as it reflects important aspects of the status of Jews in the South.

Jews in the South have given rise to many fascinating sociological studies in any number of books, articles and learned tracts. Of equal fascination, however, is how one study often contradicts another. Wayward human nature can produce statistics that don't add up and render hazardous generalities.

Two men intimately connected with the proud University of Virginia will serve to compare the sympathetic with the unsympathetic view. First its founder, Thomas Jefferson, who wrote in 1818 to a Jewish newspaper editor in New York, deploring "the prejudice that still scowls over your sect of our religion." The second its president, W. W. Thornton, who in 1890, announced (presumably with a straight face) that the reason for prejudice against Jews was that they cared less for culture than Christians of the same economic level, adding that "he had never seen a really scholarly Jewish student." He allowed that prejudice might subside if only Jews would marry Christians and accept the true faith.

In Georgia in the nineteenth century, one newspaper remarked that "the Jews possess a plentiful lot of money together with the scorn of the entire world," while another paper, also in Georgia, praised a Jewish merchant as "a typical exponent of the characteristics of his race [who] has happily exemplified that spirit of progressive enterprise which his people are noted for all over the world." Still another paper there gave a slightly backhanded welcome to some Jews newly settled in its town with "Where there are no Jews there is no money to be made."

Yet there were other services southern communities looked to the Jew to perform. In early days in the South, the Jewish peddler was not solely an object of mockery, as often depicted. Along with his wares, many Christians held him in special regard. Frequently, he was asked about the Bible and was often required to settle religious disputes because, as one said, "I was a Jew and they all looked upon me as an authority." Sometimes in rural areas he would be asked, "Are you a Baptist Jew or a Methodist Jew?"

On the other hand, there were fundamentalist preachers who forcefully preached anti-Semitism on the religious grounds that the Jews killed Christ. But there were also fundamentalist churchgoers who declared themselves close to Jews because, like them, they were schooled in the Old Testament and, therefore, shared the same religious imagery.

The smaller the town, the more intense the anti-Semitism, was the conclusion that one expert had arrived at. The humorist Harry Golden, however, comes to the opposite conclusion. The South had a history of philo-Semitism, he wrote, and in the rural South, the people held the Jewish citizenry almost as dearly as private possessions. "He is 'our Jew' to small town southerners, and they often take care of him with the zeal and devotion otherwise bestowed only on the Confederate monument in the square."

Nevertheless, anti-Semitism still dogs the southern Jew. An anti-Semitic candidate can run for a major office there without hiding his prejudice. Not too long ago the first Jew to be elected mayor of Atlanta charged that reporters and newscasters were less than friendly in referring to him as "the Jewish liberal from the synagogue district." Notwithstanding, a national survey showed that the South would be more likely to vote for a Jewish presidential candidate than the North.

Jews have lived in the South since colonial times and their descendants are still southern. They took up the Southerners' accent, the belief in the Confederacy and the belief in slavery—some owned slaves and some sold them.

More recently, many of them are deeply conflicted about civil rights: inwardly they may know that segregation is wrong, but some feel also that to proclaim this would damage their gentile friendships. These Jews are southerners first and then Americans.

Intermarrying has been not uncommon for three centuries. It generally causes Jews to disappear into non-Jewish environments. Many other Jews view this with alarm, explaining that the very absence of persecution is causing Judaism as a religion and Jews as a people to disappear. There is the story of the perfectly assimilated reform rabbi in Richmond, Virginia, handsome, robust, sophisticated and much admired by the gentile community of his town, who confessed to a friend shortly before his death, "One thing in which I have failed was in developing a following among Jews such as I have among Christians."

People forget that in the first half of the twentieth century you were obligated, if you belonged to a minority, to assimilate—to plunge into the melting pot and emerge as a WASP (or near enough). Getting into your own ethnic group came into its own only in the sixties.

When Howard K. Smith came back to Ferriday in 1977 to do a television program on the changing South, one of the first questions he asked was, "Is Pasternacks still in business?" Since it is hardly possible that as a child of three he would have stored that memory, it indicates that contact with the Pasternacks lasted for longer than the Smiths' stay in Ferriday. In fact, Wolf Pasternack bought land from Howard's father. Howard's brother remembered that his mother "loved Mrs. Pasternack. She had a flock of boys and they'd all come to dinner wearing little straw hats." The family was memorable.

Wolf and Clara Pasternack had five boys: Joe, Abe, Herman, Sam and Morris, and two girls, Rose and Freida (one of whom married a rather well-known bandleader in Memphis).

They were not the first Jews to come to Ferriday. Among those who purchased the initial lots in 1903 were Leopold Godchaux and Henry Godchaux. A Godchaux in Louisiana is like a Rothschild in France and a Lehman in New York. Later came the grocery firm of Rothschild and Lyons. Then a Mr. L. Friedler, who owned Forest Plantation near Vidalia, joined with Mr. Geisenberger in what developed into a large-volume grocery enterprise. These people originally came from Natchez.

The Pasternack migration probably began in New Orleans, proceeded then to Monroe, then to St. Joseph, then to the new town of Ferriday, where Wolf had heard the Wilks Brothers store was for sale on the corner of Louisiana Avenue and First Street. In 1913, Wolf purchased the store and made it into a dry goods store. Later on, he added hardware, and still later, he also bought a grocery store in partnership with Henry Godchaux. As these seem to have flourished from the start, the question is did the times make the Pasternacks or did they make the times? Probably the latter, as the Wilks Brothers had failed under the same conditions and the times were not all that auspicious. The boll weevil had devastated the cotton crop and the Mississippi overflowed every other year, leaving Ferriday with a backwater for several days. However, like Chennault, the Pasternacks absorbed their environment and used it to the utmost. There were plenty of trading opportunities, if you knew how to gather them in.

What Wolf and especially his oldest son, Big Joe, did was simply to build a better mousetrap. Aside from dry goods and hardware, there were building materials, gifts and household ware and a ladies' department, which branched out into womens' clothes. "The gay French capital is no longer the style center of the world," ran one of their ads in 1928, "even Paris looks to New York for real PEPPY models in womens' apparel." These peppy models were to be found, of course, at Pasternacks. There could also be found Mexican saddles, pot-bellied stoves, sterling silver tea sets, quality furniture, appliances, all varieties of camping and sporting goods equipment. It was the superiority of their stock that got people in there in the first place, but it was the superiority of their service that made people keep coming back and not trade elsewhere.

People remember the oddest things about this famous service. A war widow trying to maintain her home remembers always forgetting the name of the thingamajig she wanted to buy to, say, fix her windows and how the staff would make inspired guesses until they got it right. And, like as not, Big Joe would join in. "There were no slouches on that payroll," she says. "They acted like they really cared.

Some of the Pasternack brothers in the store in the 1920's. (*Credit: Joe Pasternack, Jr., private collection.*)

They were home folks and Pasternacks was home. You don't get that feeling at Walmart or the malls."

Pasternacks had a slogan that became familiar over the years: "Hard to find items are usually found at Pasternacks." But the store implemented another important service. If they didn't have precisely what you wanted, they would obtain it for you—no need to go elsewhere. This well-advertised fact guaranteed people from larger towns beating a path to their door. In this way, the Pasternacks created goodwill in trading centers such as New Orleans, Memphis, Chicago and New York.

With soaring aspirations, the Pasternacks used their store as an entree into diversified business enterprises and investments which would make them, in Ferriday's phrase, "millionaires many times over."

The Pasternacks were masters of communication. Wolf and Big Joe spent their working days on the floor talking with customers. It was a large store, over half a block long, and Little Joe remembers walking miles and miles every day making sure that the customers were taken care of. Only after the store was closed for the day would they retire to the back office. During their long conversational exchanges, the

Pasternacks were discovering what these farmers, railroad men, loggers and sawmill workers, and professional people were *going* to want, need and desire, and then saw to it that, when the time came, they had it.

Saturday in Ferriday meant different things to different people. The farmers who would not have been able to see their neighbors all week would come in with their horses and buggies (as late as the 1930's) to socialize. First, they would gather at McGlothin's Barber Shop, not only for a shave and a haircut and a gossip but—as many farms didn't have running water—for the showers that the McGlothins thoughtfully supplied.

It was also movie night and often dance night. Several times a year, Big Joe's wife, Agatha, would organize on Louisiana Avenue a cakewalk to raise money for the school band's uniforms. Band mothers baked cakes as prizes, local bands played, the street was chalk-marked like a large sliced cake and when the music stopped the youngsters standing in the right slice won a cake.

Helen Warden, looking back on her youth, recalls that "Saturday movies started at two, so we got there at one. If we didn't have the money for a movie, we'd stay home till five or six in the afternoon, then mother would put us all in the car and we'd go and park. Everybody did the same thing and so we'd just meet everybody uptown. And then as I grew older, they had street dances right up there in the same place in front of the bank. And every time a new store opened or there was any kind of event, they'd have a street dance and everybody just had a ball. They'd have two bands, and sometimes one would be playing one thing and the other would be playing something else."

Pasternacks store was part of the whole social center around Louisiana Avenue. It included the Arcade Theatre, the bank, the drugstore, where you could get sodas and ice cream cones, Charlie's Barbeque, where you could get a hamburger, and cafes where the grown-ups had coffee.

There was always a festive air around Pasternacks on Saturday night. The doors would stay open till two o'clock in the morning because everybody left shopping to the very last minute.

The Pasternacks seemed to have a sixth sense about whom they hired. When they came upon someone in Ferriday who seemed to have the knack, even though that person had not applied for the job, they talked him into it. Down the years, the staff was so well trained that, it was said, by Little Joe's time, the store didn't need anyone running it. It ran by itself.

As storekeepers, the Pasternacks had no equals in their realm. But how were they thought of socially? Ferriday was after all a small town with only a few Jews. Was there not an undercurrent of hostility that said, "We have to buy from you, but we don't have to like you"? Studies have shown anti-Semitism rampant in rural towns.

Sorry, wrong town.

Frances Thomas Smith, in her seventies, is a hardworking plantation owner. When she opens her huge Ford van, a burst of energy comes at you. Brisk and opinionated, she talks about Jews in general and the Pasternacks in particular.

"My grandmother married a Jewish man from Natchez. He owned the Elite Millinery. Mr. Beitman was just as much a granddaddy to me as anybody I know. For a time in Ferriday, one of our school board members was Jewish and he had no children, but he was loved as well as anybody could be loved. When Wolf Pasternack's wife, Clara, died, he married again, and Miss Rose was wonderful and she was very Jewish and lovely. You know, Jewish homes are always well run. She had beautiful meals. She'd make ice cream and call us all to come and eat ice cream.

"Father used to say, 'Don't trade with the chain stores. Trade with Pasternacks because that dollar stays at home. They're going to live here and they're going to spend their dollar back in.' They had a grocery store, too, with Mr. Godchaux, and Jitney Jungle was a chain store competition with a more diversified grocery list, but Daddy said, 'No, don't trade there.'

"During the Depression Daddy said, 'You go back to

Pasternacks because he's the one who gives credit.' Times were hard. [Big Joe] carried half this town on the payroll. No, he didn't get it all back. He earned our respect—a man that will have faith to feed families by the month. The Pasternacks helped make this town from way back."

Doris Morris, also in her seventies, heads a full measure of charitable ventures, including hospital volunteer work and church work. She has a listing in *Who's Who of American Women*. For many years, she ran a dress shop in Ferriday so successfully that she needed eleven salespeople. "The best schooling I could have gotten," she said, "was working fourteen years in the ladies' department at Pasternacks. You know, the Jewish people are very good if they like you and there's no question the Pasternacks loved Ferriday."

She worked under Abe, who said right off, "You're going to be good." He spoke Yiddish a lot to his brothers, which fascinated her and which she tried to learn. She will never forget: "One day when a customer returned something and I automatically spread the paper out to save it for another time and put the string back on the spool, Abe said, 'That's right. You save the string and we'll save the dollar.' I think I remembered that almost every day in my shop. He was teaching me not to waste anything. Not even the string."

By all accounts Big Joe was a charitable man. You could come to Big Joe about anything that happened. His advice was much sought after. He listened with a compassionate shrug of his left shoulder—a shrug that became famous in five parishes.

"Big Joe was a little bit of a man, a roly-poly man," says a Natchez friend, Marty Nathanson. "He had an open heart and an open pocketbook. He was a man of great generosity." For all that, his business acumen never deserted him. He had wide-flung political influence and a firm belief that whatever was good for Ferriday was good for Pasternacks. He was most instrumental in getting Highway 15 built. They called it Pasternack's Road because he manipulated it so that it went through Ferriday and avoided Vidalia. He was a charter member of the Rotary Club and chairman of the Red Cross. He was a member of many clubs and lodges, always widening his horizons and extending his scope of influence. Certainly the knowledge that in other towns these organizations would be forbidden to Jews must have given him an added incentive to succeed.

When the Mississippi River overflowed in 1927, it did not miss Ferriday. But people in their boats rowing around the town were cheered by a sign on the non-immersed part of Pasternacks saying, "Noah stood it. So can we."

A recurrent theme in studies of southern anti-Semitism reveals that it frequently goes hand in hand with anti-Italian, anti-Catholic feeling.

Coincident with the founding of the town of Ferriday, a rash of anti-Italian incidents broke out which led to lynchings in New Orleans, Hahnville, Tallulah and elsewhere on the Mississippi River.

In Ferriday, one of the first people to buy lots was the Italian-American Tony Brocato, who, with his family, enjoyed a peaceful existence there for the rest of his life. His descendents are still in Ferriday. Gloria, a grandchild who

Pasternack's takes a gallant stand during the flood of 1927. (*Credit: Joe Pasternack, Jr., private collection.*)

was once homecoming queen in high school, runs the oldest and best restaurant in town. Her brother is a deputy sheriff. A great many other Italians have come to settle in both Ferriday and Vidalia, and a glance at either local paper yields any number of Italian names active in civic affairs. An imposing integrated Catholic Church has a large congregation.

It is a wry comment on human nature that people hearing of this absence of anti-Semitism and anti-Catholicism in Ferriday always express surprise. It seems remarkable to them that one group of Americans can treat another group as if they, too, were Americans. However, not despising or fearing their neighbors, not shouldering the heavy burden of hatred, freed the citizens of Ferriday to concentrate on truly doing their own thing.

Big Joe's closest friend was Lawrence Alwood, who was the nephew of none other than Elmer Porter, the train engineer turned plantation owner. Needing help to cope with the large plantation, Delhi, he had sent for his sister and his son-in-law, Minnie and Charles Alwood, who had been farmers in Illinois and had to get used to the South and southern farming. Mrs. Alwood, a fiery temperance woman, never got used to living in the South. Charles Alwood got off to a bad start by insisting on planting cotton on flat ground the way he planted things up North, but the better Charles got at managing Delhi, the more it seemed to Elmer that he really preferred living in town where he could be close to his cherished trains than stuck on a big farm, so he and his wife, Fanny, moved back to Ferriday.

After Charles, his son Lawrence, a planter and cattleman, became so adept at managing Delhi that when Elmer died he bequeathed it to Lawrence in his will. Lawrence was eight years younger than Big Joe. What they had in common, this archetype of a merchant prince and this archetype of landed gentry, besides an obsession with bridge (Big Joe and his wife, Agatha, and Lawrence and his wife, Pauline, were dedicated to the game and played together as often as they could), was a deep sense of *noblesse oblige,* and each reinforced the other in this sentiment. Together, they planned to do something enduring for Ferriday, something worthy of their stature as town benefactors.

When they wanted to present to the town was a large ring levee that would encircle Concordia Parish, releasing it from the floodings that yearly rendered thousands of acres useless. Who would pay for this costly dream of a levee plus a pumping station? Their answer was another dream, federal funds.

Big Joe and Lawrence had been the earliest supporters of Louisiana Congressman Otto Passman. With every re-election, Passman had gained power in the House. He was a good friend of Richard Nixon and, most importantly, headed Congress's Appropriations Committee. He was all for the levee. Big Joe and Alwood began entertaining politically influential people for all they were worth. Richard Alwood, Lawrence's son, remembers a period of elaborate cocktail parties at the plantation held every weekend for top brass engineers and politicians.

They got the levee and the pumping station. And—not miraculously—they got the federal grant. It changed the outlook in Ferriday.

Big Joe was always Santa Claus in Ferriday's Christmas parade. It was an act that must have been satisfyingly symbolic to the Ferridians, one that reaffirmed his mythic position in the town, an act that joined all religions in the season of goodwill, an act as appropriate as the candy he threw to the children as he went by.

Big Joe worked twelve to fourteen hours every day till the day he died. At sixty-seven, in 1963, he was driving around with Lawrence overseeing some construction on the levee. He had a heart attack and died, virtually in Lawrence's arms.

Big Joe's funeral was an event attended by people from miles around. Traffic was blocked for hours and finally had to be rerouted. Services were held in Ferriday's largest Baptist church. Officiating were a rabbi, a Catholic priest

Big Joe Pasternack as Santa Claus, 1960. (*Credit: Joe Pasternack, Jr.,
private collection.*)

and Methodist, Baptist and Presbyterian ministers. Family,
friends, customers, employees and passers-by, visibly moved
and audibly weeping, made the occasion memorable.

Marty Nathanson is a New York lawyer transplanted to
Natchez. In his late seventies, he has a real estate office in
Vidalia, teaches at Alcorn State University and entertains on
the piano with selections of show tunes at various restaurants. He echoes studies of the disappearing Jew in small
southern towns. It was not on account of prejudice. According to him, there has been very little religious prejudice in
the area. "In fact, there was hardly a thing that took place
that the Jewish people weren't involved in. I think the non-
Jewish people feel worse about the death of the Jewish
community than even the Jews do. But the Jewish people in
this area have either intermarried or died off. No new ones
came in. There is nothing here to attract a Jewish person.
There's no job they want.

"We at one time had a very large Jewish community in
Natchez and the outlying areas. We have this beautiful
synagogue that seats over 350 people [where Ferriday's Jews
would go to worship]. Last night for services, we had eleven
people, and that was large. In 1972, our last rabbi passed

away, and to keep the congregation going, I had to conduct the services. I'm not in any way official, but I had to keep the Jewish congregation alive. Now we have a rabbinical student who comes in from the seminary in Cincinnati one weekend a month and in the High Holidays. He has all kinds of meetings with the sick and so on. A month from now he'll come back to conduct the services."

—————

Little Joe, now in his fifties, has a very different personality from Big Joe. Where Big Joe was overflowing, Little Joe is very much what businessmen are like today—compact, contained and collected. He managed the store for twenty years and closed it in 1983. Some say it was because he and his sister, Betty Claire, don't see eye to eye, but most say, "What's the point? There's a Walmart in Ferriday or we can easily go to Natchez, and, anyway, there are any number of chain stores on the highway."

Little Joe now lives in a suburb of New Orleans with his wife and son, Joe III. But he keeps a house on Lake St. John.

The Joe Pasternack, Jrs., with son, Joe Pasternack III. (*Credit: Joe Pasternack, Jr., private collection.*)

"Closing the store," he says, "was like a death in the family."

Big Joe loved show business and always used show business expressions, especially in connection with the store. He found reassurance in the phrase, "The show must go on," and used it often. He would arrange goods in the store as if he were staging a production.

In those early settlements up the Mississippi River where the Italians went into the restaurant and grocery businesses and the Jews into dry goods, hardware, and clothing stores, the Jews also in the early days of the twentieth century inaugurated movie houses.

The movies, from their inception, played an important role in the town of Ferriday, as they did all over the world. Howard Smith's brother, Prescott, vividly remembered that there was a picture show in Ferriday back in the teens, where he used to see Pearl White. The man who ran the picture show was Sol Boyar, who also had a clothing store down by the depot. Not much is known about him except the fact of his existence and the existence of his pretty daughter, who was born in Biloxi and who was called Ann. His name and the businesses he owned make it highly probable that he was Jewish, though, on the other hand, he may not have been.

Pretty little Ann Boyar grew up to be a woman of extraordinary beauty. A photographic portrait taken in the late 1930's shows her with glossy black hair, huge, luminous, mascaraed eyes under imperially arched eyebrows and a small, exquisitely painted, sexy mouth. Her expression says, "I am too beautiful to need an expression," and she was right. The photograph was her husband's favorite. He was Jack Warner of Warner Brothers.

First she married a movie actor, Don Alvarado (whose real last name was Page) and next she married Jack Warner. The beautiful Mrs. Warner was not content with being a Hollywood wife, which in those days meant shopping, cards and seeing your psychiatrist. She stepped out and became a legendary hostess and leader in international society. She

had palaces in Hollywood and Palm Springs and an apartment
at the Sherry Netherland in New York. Salvador Dali, impressed with her beauty, painted her portrait. Writer Richard Gully says, "I always thought of her as a Southern belle."
He escorted her once to Paris and remembers that it was her
patronage that launched the couturier Pierre Balmain, who
in honor of Ann created his most popular perfume, Jolie
Madame. She died recently, and Richard Gully writes in
tribute: "Ann Warner was royalty. She looked like a queen;
she lived like a queen. God bless her."

After Sol Boyar and the silent films came Morris Meltz,
who took over the Arcade Theatre on Louisiana Avenue and
called it the Meltz Arcade. With Meltz, Ferriday had a full-
blown cineast in its midst. In the 1930's and 1940's, movies
were big. It was the era of the big western and the big
musical, and Morris chose to run the best of them and as
many of them as possible. Mrs. Ben Green, one of whose
many jobs was to be the ticket seller, comments on how nice
it was for Ferriday to have a serious movie enthusiast. "He
changed the program real often. The best picture he'd run
on Sunday and Monday. Then Tuesday was western day,
then Wednesday and Thursday he'd have something else real
good, a musical or a comedy, and Saturday matinees had all
the western serials. He had all the big Jimmy Stewart
pictures and all the John Wayne and John Ford ones. There
never was a picture show anywhere around that had better
movies than we did, and they were all well attended." In the
flood of 1945, when the water rose twelve feet in Ferriday,
Meltz kept the Arcade open so that people could row to the
movies in their boats and sit in them while watching the
movie.

"Mr. Meltz never married," says Mrs. Green, "I think
his family came from Russia. He was a highly educated man
and loved good music. He was so loyal to the town that all he
wanted to do was better everything. He was a bachelor and
his only brother had died. When he died, he left everything
to the Ferriday children." All his money went into scholarships, into an athletic field for Ferriday High still called

Meltz Field, and for a while the yearbook, which was called
The Meltzer.

"After Mr. Meltz died in the early fifties, one of the
chains bought the Arcade. They just didn't have any interest
in it. It was never the same."

Says Doris Morris, "When the Jews leave a town, it just
wilts."

THE FERRIDAY THREE —
PART ONE
JERRY LEE LEWIS

To the rest of the world, the Deep South is a foreign country. It is perceived as primitive, barbarous, explosive, exotic and isolated. In its contradictory fashion, it is seen as both highly literate and deeply ignorant, as cowardly and heroic. It also produces a disproportionate amount of very famous men and women. It is inhabited by people larger than life, eccentric, colorful, overdramatic, in fact, downright theatrical. Hiram "Pete" Gregory, born and raised in Ferriday, Professor of Anthropology at Northwestern University at Natchitoches, explains the phenomenon: "Southerners are colorful and eccentric because their parents and grandparents were. It's their way of defending themselves in the family situation."

In the Swaggart-Lewis-Gilley clan, it was not enough for the young cousins, Jimmy, Jerry Lee and Mickey, born six months apart, 1935 to 1936, to be colorful and eccentric, they must compete with each other as well and, of equal importance, so must their mothers. The air was rife with sibling rivalry. Jimmy's and Jerry Lee's mothers were sisters, while Mickey's mother was sister to Jerry Lee's father and to

Jimmy's grandmother. Add to the brew that they were all born with great musical and histrionic talent, with the need to gain attention and the magnetism to hold it, and it is no wonder that there were some pretty uncommon goings-on around Mississippi Avenue and Third Street in Ferriday.

What is so extraordinary about these cousins, the Ferriday Three, is that they so perfectly embody the mythic figures that come to mind when we conjure up Crazy Rock Star or Fallen Preacher or Easygoing Country Singer, as they live out their symbolic lives. In Freudian terms, these cousins could constitute a whole organism, with Jimmy Swaggart as the super-ego, Mickey Gilley as the ego, and Jerry Lee Lewis as the id. With these three, this small town can tell the whole story about a large part of contemporary American culture: a culture that is not only exported to the rest of our country but to the rest of the world.

The children were tied in a filial knot that bound them together very tightly. It produced a climate of behavior that Frankie Terrell, sister of Jerry Lee, looks back on in this way.

> You try to find a role to play in the family that's comfortable and you struggle for that role. And you're looked at strange. And you look back at them strange. Everything's so strange. And everybody's talking. Everybody's making their best recipe. Everybody's doing their best singing. Everybody's doing their best playing. Everybody's doing their best baking. Everybody's making their best bedspread. Everyone is trying to compete their children with each other, pushing their children and pushing their children and the children are all there and "Oh mine can sing. Have you heard the new song he did? Did you see the way he walks? Did you see the hair on his arms? It's perfect. My children do not wash dishes. Do you see their piano fingers?"
>
> And it went on with church. Whoever sang the song that brought down the power, that divine power, where everyone would start to speak in tongues and cry and receive a blessing, then that was the person that had them under their spell. The power would shift. Jerry a very few times would sing and the power would go into the people. A very few times. He would leave the church and he would

say, "Mama," (he would deny this if he hears it, but it's so true), he would say, "Mama, why is that when Frankie sings they all clap and get so emotional? How does that come around? How does she move them like that?" *I* said, "Well, Jerry, it's because it's from the heart. That's how I did it. Because I'm no phony." I said, "I am a true Christian," and he got so angry he turned white—just ashy white.

If Jerry Lee is the most interviewed piano player in the world, Frankie is the most interviewed sister. Like all the clan, she has, if not the eccentricity of genius, a genius for eccentricity.

One of a kind, Frankie, born in 1943, now married with five children, does her household chores by candlelight in bright daytime. When ironing, she will eye the candle; when it has burned down to a certain level, she will blow it out, put up the iron and take a break. When rested, she will light the candle and go back to work again. It is her way of freeing herself from the despotism of the inexorably ticking clock.

During her rest, Frankie talks about the mothers who were in head-on competition about the church, who was holier than who, more strenuously saved, more active in spreading the word, more vigorously born again and more overflowing with the Holy Spirit. The mothers also made it clear that their sons would be held responsible for their mothers' position on the social ladder.

A word should be said about southern mothers. These strong-willed women are serenely accustomed to the obedience of their sons, whom they have molded into shameless mother-worshipers for the rest of their lives. When they are young mothers, they begin unabashedly flirting with their sons, who unabashedly flirt back. To a stranger this may seem overtly sexual (as it is), but the fact that it is the done thing all through the South staves off any adverse comment. Mothers are constantly hugging and squeezing and kissing their little boys. They also give them whisperings—cuddling them in their laps and whispering to them what great men they will grow up to be and how proud they're going to make their mamas. The end product is the boy-man who, overflow-

Frankie Lewis Terrell, Jerry Lee's sister, her husband, Marion, and her two youngest children. "It's portrait time, girls," she said, "it's straight up time."
(*Credit: Rhett Powell.*)

ing with gratitude, "does it all for his mother's sake" and can never do enough. Explains Mickey, "I didn't make it as easy as I should have for my mother. Regardless of what I'd done for her, I don't think I'd have been satisfied."

When their prayers have been answered a hundred-fold by their sons' successes, the mothers sit back and accept their fame and fortune as only their due and say, "Didn't I always tell you it would happen, son?" And continue ordering them around.

When you ask men over fifty living in Ferriday about their mothers, you will see "that look." Their faces open, relax and soften. Their voices soften too. But don't expect them to utter phrases of banal sentimentality about her, for what emerges from their memories of their mothers is amusement—a positive merriment—as they recount how stubborn and funny she was and how she always got her own way. Austin Wilson tells of his mother visiting him on Grand

Isle, off New Orleans. An elderly woman, she had to use a
cane to walk. There was a storm brewing and storm warnings
had been broadcast. Helicopters at the nearby airport were
ready, if necessary, and Austin said they'd wait and see
which way the storm was heading. His mother exploded.
"I've never seen anything so idiotic in my life. Just sitting
there and letting your children drown." Flinging away her
cane, she tucked a grandchild under each arm and strode
out to the nearby airfield. Sam Hanna, the feared, revered
editor and publisher of Ferriday's *Concordia Sentinel,* when
asked about his mother, simply reached into the top drawer
of his desk, pulling out letters and snapshots of her that he's
kept there since he took over the office and will keep there
forever.

Inside the mothers of each of our cousins was a tomboy,
a circumstance directly connected with growing up in rural
poverty, where being able to pick cotton with the best of
them was as important as climbing trees or commandeering
the family's Model-T and risking the safety of the town's
population by teaching themselves to drive. Jerry Lee's
mother, throughout her life, loved to ride a motorcycle.

Mickey's mother, Irene, besides being a genuinely devout
and kind woman, had a strong streak of the tomboy in her.
Mickey remembers:

> My father was a hell raiser and a womanizer. My mother
> knew it. I remember on one occasion when I was eight
> years old, I had been working on my bicycle to get the
> kickstand back on it and then I got into the back seat of
> our old 1939 Mercury with my parents. My mother and
> father were arguing. I will never forget my mother accus-
> ing him of running around. Anyway, my dad was in this
> argument with my mom and she said something about how
> nice he kept up the car and how she wished he'd keep our
> house up as well. And he said, "I beautify my car to ride
> my women in." So then my dad got out of the car and
> started to walk to town, and no sooner had he rounded the
> corner when she said, "Mickey, get out of the car." And
> all the windows were rolled up and I got out. And she
> grabbed my kickstand and swung it and beat every window
> out all the way around. My father had to drive that car

down through town to get all the windows put back in. It was gorgeous. He had it painted.

And I remember, on another occasion, that my mother went down to my father's place of business, and there was this old gal that Daddy had been messing around with. Mama pulled a gun out of her purse and took a shot at her. I have no idea why they didn't put her in jail for attempted murder. When I would bring it up, my mother would just get red-faced and say, "Son, I can't believe you're talking like that." And I'd say, "Mama, you did it. I didn't do it. You did it." And she said, "I've had to repent for that many times, son. That was a sin, that was wrong," and I'd get her to laugh.

An important way that members of a family communicate is by teasing. This only appears to be a light-hearted activity. In fact, it enables mothers and sons to practice a thousand little cruelties or jollities on each other between breakfast and dinner. Teasing, in fact, may be said to characterize a relationship.

With Mickey and his mother, it was a sharpish but essentially good-natured pastime, as in Mickey's reminding her of her rambunctious past. And Mickey recalls that he was half-joking, half-serious when he would say to her, "Mom, if you don't like what I do, don't pray against me. Just pray for me to be a better person, but don't pray against what I'm doing." Or giving her $500 and teasing, "Mama, I'm giving you some money but I want you to spend it on *yourself.*" To which Irene would reply, "I'm going to give ten percent of it to the Lord. You know that." "Hour Magazine," a television program, had Mickey and his mother as guests. Irene, in her eighties, made cornbread on it as calmly as if she'd been on television forever. Mickey stood in the background, grinning and occasionally coming forward to hug her.

With Mamie, teasing the grown-up Jerry Lee often took the form of twisting in a knife. In the past, she gave her all-out devotion, but now she adjusted her style and took to telling him that whoever was his latest wife was an adulteress and a slut. Pointedly, she would carry around his arch-rival

Chuck Berry's record, "Little Queenie," playing it morning, noon and night, until finally Jerry Lee gave in, called a session at Sun Studios and recorded it himself for her.

Minnie Bell, since giving herself to the Lord and Son's supervision, had undergone a transformation. Once a cute, curvy coquette with fashionable marcelled hair and a bright lipsticked mouth, she turned into a plain, subdued figure, wearing unbecoming rimless glasses through which she looked at the world with a quiet fanaticism. If Irene's Christianity released her to happiness, Minnie Bell's seems to have had a troubling effect on her. With Jimmy, she had that soft and persistent way of teasing, which often tipped over into nagging. When Jimmy rejected the church in his teens, she would come home after a revival and pray over him in his bedroom. Later, she would say time and again, "God has called you since you were a child." That was to keep him in line. And when she felt he wasn't giving his all, she would say of God, "He has much better things for you in store than this. Now give the ministry all the strength and energy you have."

The three mothers approached their church from three different directions. Jerry's mother may be said to have employed the Assembly of God Church as a try-out stage for her talented children, especially for Jerry Lee to display his extraordinary gifts on the piano. For Jimmy's mother, Minnie Bell, now that Son was a full-time preacher, she was intent on making second-generation preachers of both Jimmy and his younger sister, Jeanette. For Mickey's mother, Irene, being saved was a beautiful salvation and one she badly needed. Apart from church meetings and revivals, she often held morning prayer meetings in her house. She became what the Assembly of God called an "intercessor" and a "prayer warrior," who spent many hours in prayer at home and in the church. She became, say all who knew her, a happy Christian, often giving vent to her emotions and shouting at the top of her voice and doing a beautiful holy dance to the Lord.

As children, the cousins lived in a world made marvelous by miracles.

There was Ada Swaggart, one of Jimmy's grandmothers, who had been sickly all her life. "She had taken a boxcar load of patent medicine," according to Jimmy's father, Son, "trying out everything she heard of." Then, she started going to camp meetings and revivals. She read in the Bible, "I am the Lord that heals thee of all thy diseases," and from then on, Ada's health was better than at any time of her life. She became a devotee of camp meetings. She roamed far and wide to find them.

She proved an inspiration to Jimmy, who has written, "Before she became a Christian, like the rest of the Swaggarts, she enjoyed drinking, smoking and a little gambling." At forty-five, she returned from a camp meeting one day a totally different person. She had been "anointed" by the Holy Spirit and she had spoken in tongues. With the zeal of a convert, she herself began preaching to everyone in earshot.

Young Jimmy was often in her house. He thrilled to the story of her anointing and often begged her to repeat it. She told him of her standing outside a tabernacle near a grove of trees praying, when suddenly the presence of the Lord struck her. It was like being struck by a bolt of lightning and she fell flat on her back. She began to praise the Lord, but no English came out, only unknown tongues. Whenever she got to this part of the story, "The power of God would hit her again and she'd begin speaking in tongues." Jimmy would catch the spirit too and begin crying.

There was another grandmother, Arilla Lewis. Says Son, "I baptized her myself. She was brought back from the dead. She'd had a stroke and was in the hospital. The doctor pulled the sheet over her head. The preacher was there and all the loved ones, because they knew she was dying." But their prayers brought her back to life. Frankie elaborates. "They said it was no hope, and her sisters and daughters and my mother all prayed and never stopped praying. The doctor said, "She's gone, that's it," pulled the sheet over her head. Later Arilla told me she felt she was going into a deep hole, but the prayers pulled her back, like gravity. And then, someone saw the sheet moving. And she was alive. So when she got well, she became a Christian. She said God had given her a second chance and she was always a Christian after that."

Arilla was also a great-aunt to young Pete Gregory. She was always taking him aside and asking him to preach a sermon to her. Pete, being Catholic, declined.

There were other miracles. Or perhaps witchcraft. It haunted Frankie all her life until she went to a psychiatrist with it. "Teresa Herron, another grandmother, was insane," she says. "She was declared legally incompetent and placed in an insane asylum. It was a terrible place where she was so badly beaten that my mother and Aunt Stella brought her home. We took turns. One week she was with us, the next with another and so on. I was about nine years old. The week she was with us was a living hell. She cursed, ranted and raved. She threw rocks at my school bus and the children would jeer at me all day. She was a wonderful person before, but she went out into another world and didn't come back until she died.

"I consulted this black woman who said, 'Well, she's quite old and she's in a lot of pain. It's time for her to die.' And she said, 'Bring me nail clippings from her toes and a piece of hair.' And I did. And Grandma Teresa died about a month later, and I cried because I had done it. And I didn't close my eyes for three months, thinking of her. Much later when I saw a psychiatrist, he laughed until he cried. He said, 'You're okay. That very thing happened to me as a child too.' It was voodoo, of course. I didn't understand about all of that."

For Jimmy, there was a succession of miracles. At the age of eight in 1945, he prophesied the dropping of the atom bomb, while at a prayer meeting at an aunt's house. He received another prophesy around then when God told him he would minister in large auditoriums to thousands of people. Around that time, God also talked to him as he was standing in line to go to a cowboy movie at the Meltz Arcade. "Do not go into this place, but give your heart to me. I have chosen you a vessel to be used in my service." He obeyed. He went home to the kitchen and told his mama he hadn't gone to the movie because he gave his heart to the Lord and was not going any more. Minnie Bell cried, overjoyed. Jimmy felt "good and clean, almost like taking a bath continuously." A song seemed to bubble in his heart.

In his early days as an itinerant preacher, Jimmy traveled in an old Plymouth, which one day broke down completely. Jimmy got out of the car and prayed to the Lord to heal it. It recovered. When Jerry Lee gave him a brand-new Oldsmobile, it was in answer to many months of praying for it.

Most welcome miracle of all, God removed in a flash Jimmy's terrible sinus headaches and sinus blocks that had tormented him for four years.

———

There is one image of their childhoods that should claim our attention. It is of Jimmy and Jerry Lee at eight and nine going into the woods behind their houses and praying so loud you could hear them for blocks away. There they stayed for hours, telling people afterward they were having visions and revelations.

There is a glorious innocence to these capers. The odd conduct of many adherents of the Assembly of God must have frightened as well as impressed these children, and they were turning it all into fun and play. And who knows? Perhaps they did have a bright vision or two. In India, boys of their age are considered soaring spiritual vessels. Those who have the calling get their heads shaved, don saffron robes and become boy Buddhists.

In Ferriday, boys of that age played cowboys and Indians and cops and robbers. But eight-year-olds playing loud supplicants, playing visionary saints exulting in revelations, shows a degree of spiritual commitment to the church that began very young and that would last throughout their lives. Lee Calhoun thought someone should take a belt to them.

When Jerry Lee was sixteen and already married to his second wife, he enrolled in Southwestern Bible Institute in Waxahachie, Texas, to become a preacher. That he only stayed three months—he was asked to leave for playing hymns with a boogie beat—is indicative of his refusal to obey authority rather than his indifference to his religion, for upon leaving, he went straight to the Assembly of God Church and began preaching.

In 1970, with two major upheavals in his life—Myra, his third wife, married to him twelve years, beginning divorce proceedings and his cherished mother seriously ill—he turned to Ferriday, his church and his kin. Back in 1956, in spite of his burgeoning fame accompanied by money, it was no accident that he chose to live in Memphis at the very modest home of his cousin J. W. Brown, who was part of his trio, and that he married Brown's daughter Myra. She was thirteen and he felt he could mold her, but even more important was the fact that she was a cousin. With his fame came notoriety, as scary to him as it was heady. Whom could he trust and feel comfortable with but his kin?

As for Mamie, in 1970 a doctor in Houston diagnosed her as having cancer. According to Jerry Lee in an interview with a British journalist, he brought Mamie back to Ferriday "with no more than a few weeks to live," he held a church revival meeting at the Assembly of God, and came forward and promised the Lord he'd turn his music to Him and give up life on the road and sing only gospel.

An extraordinary album (unreleased 1970), recorded live in a church with its choir in the background, has Jerry Lee flinging himself into gospel as wholeheartedly as he did into rock. He talks a great deal and most revealingly between the songs, telling his audience that he's been saved now "for two and a half weeks," that there is nothing like the great Christian songs, that all "I want to be is at a good revival and talk about Jesus," that "I been all over the world making money and I can tell you money just don't make you happy. Jesus makes you happy." And very often, as in "Amazing Grace," he expresses himself in the third person, substituting "Was blind but now I see," with "But right now old Jerry Lee can see."

At this time, Walter Cronkite, on his evening news report, announced that Jerry Lee was giving up rock for gospel, further, that he promised to devote his life and talent to God and give all his money to his church. He would cancel his shows. He would never set foot in a nightclub again. And he didn't for six months. His mother went back to Houston and the doctors could find no trace of the cancer. At his next public engagement, he sang gospel and was resoundingly booed.

Eventually, he drifted back to the honky-tonks. Mamie fell ill again with cancer and died not long after that.

———

"Mother told us all we were perfect," recalls Frankie. "Maybe she gave us some serious hang-ups, but we loved it at the time. She'd say to us, 'Look at your backs, look at the way you walk. I can tell my children fifteen miles away because you're so different.' Then she'd say to one of the other mothers, 'Oh God, how wonderfully my children sing and play.' Then she'd get us ready for another talent show."

Predictably, young Jimmy and Mickey were roped into the act. When Jerry Lee was nine, his father bought him a Stark upright piano by mortgaging the house and, also predictably, after that, Jimmy got a piano, and after that, Mickey got a piano, too.

"The day of the talent show," continued Frankie, "my parents would pick cotton all day, and I would keep my baby sister, Linda, quiet on a blanket under a tree, and Jerry Lee would be riding his bike all over Ferriday just to let everybody see him. And at the end of the day, my parents would take those huge long sacks of cotton they picked, get it weighed up and get paid. And they'd get Jerry set up for the night. Get gas for the car and get his new clothes. Get food for him after the show—the show came first—we ate afterward. They'd go to Monroe and Natchez. Everything was pressed. Everything had to match back then. Everything was so starched and ironed, and our car was always new and shiny and mostly Jerry would wear a bow tie. Linda and I, all starched and pressed, looked like little fashion queens."

A sudden lurch of memory reminds her of her favorite dress as a child. "It was just a frilly little dress that my mother had someone sew for me, and Mother had put on this extra lace. I loved lace, still do. And she just put lace everywhere until it looked really silly. It was a very lacy little

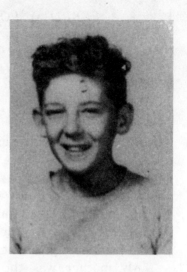

Young Jerry Lee Lewis: school days.
(*Credit: Roy Turner private collection.*)

dress, and I wore it to church every Sunday. It was pink. At
the edge of the skirt, she put rows of lace. It was ridiculous
but it was beautiful. She would add things to it. I wore it till
I outgrew it. I think I might have that dress somewhere
stashed in my attic. But Mother had only one dress. That
black dress. She wore it all the time and it was always clean
and neat. I have the buttons. I purchased a little display case
and I put the buttons in that case. They're not buttons we
have today. They're rhinestone, in a cufflink style with a
sidebar. They're precious buttons. Still it was only one dress.
They say unselfish mothers make very selfish children."

Frankie illustrates that with an example. "In the early
sixties, my parents broke up. My father wanted a divorce to
marry a young girl. My mother was so crushed she went into
a deep depression and was bedridden for two years. Then,
she found a man she loved. And Jerry threw him out. It was
okay for Jerry to play around and for Jerry to have 300 wives
or half a dozen but not his mother. Heaven forbid. Jerry said
to her, 'I take care of you. I gave you your house. There's no
need for another man. You have drapes that cost so much you
could hang hundred dollar bills up instead of them.' Jerry
always pointed out what he'd done for you—that's men. So
Mother's boyfriend gave her an ultimatum. Linda was living
with her at the time and the place he wanted them to stay
was very meek and humble. Nothing that Mother had been

used to for a long time. Anyway, Jerry Lee would not accept
him and ordered him out, and it broke Mother's heart."

———

In the 1940's, young Jerry Lee won just about every talent
contest he entered. He was getting known on the talent
contest circuit as a winner. And then his cousins joined him
and he would play duets with Cousin Jimmy. Then, for a
while, Cousin Mickey would play duets with Jerry Lee, too.
On radio shows in Natchez sometimes there would be Jerry
Lee on piano, Jimmy on accordion and Mickey on guitar.

"My mother was the leader of the other two," says
Frankie. It was Mamie this and Mamie that, that's all you
ever heard. She had the gift of gab, and she'd get everybody
socially involved. Everybody went to Mamie's to eat. Even if
they didn't like her, they would still come by to see her, find
out what she had to say. They loved to come and sit there
and talk and be with her in her presence. She'd talk about
different movie stars, talk about the country we lived in and
the things she liked to do. But the real hardcore conversation
just involved the clan because it was about their children.
The other mothers would say to her, 'What's your advice?
Should we take Mickey someplace or other?' Mother would
tell her what to wear. And they always would bring the kids
over and say, 'Well, how do you think they look for this
audition?' And all the men worshipped Mother and wanted
to dance with her. Mother was having all the parties, and all
the Christmas doings and the decorations, it was always at
Mother's. Though Mickey's mother, Irene, was number one
in religion. Mother thought Irene could just play a harp.
They were always getting recipes from Mamie. She was
extremely overpowering. She would take Linda, my younger
sister, and get her dressed, and Linda would be, like,
petrified before the show, going on stage. We went to every
damn talent show you could think of and Linda would be five
years old and saying, 'I can't, I can't,' and Mother would say,
'Yes, you can.' And Linda would. Mother never had any
stardom, but Mother had Linda.

"And all she wanted from me was for me to sing and perform. I hated it but if she were alive today, I'd perform, you know, if it would make her happy."

Then there were other sessions with Mamie, Minnie Bell, Ida and Aunt Irene. "They'd all get together and get their children together and do a brainwashing scheme on us. They'd get us together and talk about things that we shouldn't do. They said if we had sex, we would make a glow or something and that would reveal us. We'd walk outside and everyone in the town would know. They said, 'Remember when you burned your finger on the stove? That's hell. If you say those cuss words, if you steal, if you lie, if you let a man touch you.' I tried to walk out and I'd get brought back and spanked. I thought I wasn't listening until I got married and the next day I wouldn't go to church. I said I'll be damned if I'm going to church and everyone's going to know I've had sex."

———

"I taught Jimmy everything he knows," Jerry Lee has been fond of saying down through the ages, "I taught him how to preach. I was quite a preacher myself at one time. I taught Mickey everything he knows, too. I gave him 'Room Full of Roses.' I spoiled them boys rotten. There's only one thing I didn't teach them. How to rock." (It was, of course, Ferriday's famous Haney's Big House that had taught him how to rock.) Or, again about his cousins, in slightly different words, "I think Mickey's had it. He and Jimmy, they don't have the depth I have. I got all the talent. They just got the scrapings."

Graceless as these utterances may sound, it has to be conceded that he is right up to a point. It did begin with Jerry Lee. They did learn from him and he did help them. He was the first of these poor, obscure young nobodies to achieve fame and success. He was their trailblazer. What he doesn't say is how much it hurts when they surpass him.

In 1954, when Roger Bannister ran the mile in under four minutes, though no one had done it before, suddenly everyone was doing it because they knew it could be done.

Just so it might be said when Jerry Lee had his first record "Crazy Arms" played on the air and was on his way to becoming rich and famous, he broke the sound barrier for Jimmy and Mickey, and they could try it. And what Jimmy and Mickey must have felt about it all, besides their natural feelings of envy, were the more useful feelings of inspiration, encouragement and family pride.

In 1957, on the Steve Allen show, Jerry Lee exploded with the comedic talent of a young Danny Kaye, whom he resembled physically, long and thin, with flashing fingers and an unruly mop of hair. It was like watching electricity in a high wind. Of the eighty-eight notes on a piano, he seemed to play all of them in every number. Like Elvis, overnight he became a five-Cadillac man and, like Elvis, relatives' hands were immediately extended to receive. Jerry Lee gave freely, as he does to this day, making himself available for fund-raisers in Ferriday's school system. It was Jerry Lee, not Jimmy, who recently paid for the air conditioning system in the Assembly of God Church on Texas Street.

Tupelo, Mississippi, and Ferriday, Louisiana, are 298 miles apart, but in 1935, each small town gave birth to one of the most important figures in rock and roll.

Being born in the same year wasn't all that Elvis Presley and Jerry Lee Lewis would have in common. The similarities in the young lives of the two poor white southerners is astonishing. Both Elvis and Jerry were three years old when their fathers were in prison. Both fathers later on got work building other prisons. Each had an older relative who made moonshine. Each had experienced the loss of an older brother, though Elvis's older twin died at birth, and Jerry Lee's brother died when he was three.

The Assembly of God Church, which they both attended, had a seminal influence on their beliefs in God, in the Holy Spirit and in an audience. It is where each first learned to sing.

They both adored and were adored by their mothers. Though Gladys, Elvis's mother, saw to it that he finished

high school and learned manners, implicit in Mamie's attitude toward school was that it really had nothing to teach
Jerry Lee, who quit at fourteen.

Both had an all-embracing love of black music, and both
had close proximity to it in growing up, Jerry Lee at Haney's
Big House in Ferriday, and Elvis on Beale Street in Memphis.

Both Jerry and Elvis, while still in their teens, became
the main breadwinners of their families and remained so.

When Jerry Lee came to Memphis, it was to Sam Phillips
of Sun Records that he headed to follow in the footsteps of
Elvis, who had made both himself and the Sun label famous.
And it was Lansky's, favored clothing store of black musicians, that they both patronized. Between the two of them,
the voice of the poor white South, sounding like its black
neighbors, would be heard for the first time.

One of the things Jerry Lee cannot deal with even now is
his feeling of jealousy for Elvis, the phantom King and his
still-vast kingdom of teens of all ages.

Back in 1958, when Elvis was drafted into the army, it
was thought he would lose his public, and it was speculated
that Jerry Lee would become the new King. The English
press thought so and the red welcoming carpet was laid out
for him on his arrival in England in the spring of that year.
When it was uncovered that he had married his third wife,
Myra, who was thirteen years old and his cousin, there was
a great outcry. He was called a cradle-snatching bigamist. A
mere technicality, said Jerry Lee. He was divorced from his
second wife, but she hadn't quite gotten divorced from him,
or rather, it was his first wife he hadn't been divorced from
properly. Members of Parliament freely gave their opinions,
the Home Office joined in, concerts were canceled and Jerry
Lee and his wife left.

For Jerry Lee and his career, the bottom had fallen out
and he had fallen through. American radio and TV networks
and concert halls would show him the same hostility that
Britain did, and it would last for ten years. The crown eluded
him forever.

But the truth is that Jerry Lee never would have been
King. He lacked that one essential quality: romance. Though

on the face of it, his life could certainly be called romantic in its Byronic excesses, he was not able to translate this into his persona. Jerry Lee's performances promised the teens sex; but Elvis promised them sex and romance—and mystery. Elvis was able also to expose that quality of vulnerability in himself that audiences need to take a performer to their hearts. Jerry Lee scorned such weakness, preferring arrogance.

Who is the real Jerry Lee? The outlaw braggart who glories in his misdeeds or the terrified sinner living a hell on earth, God-bitten and bedeviled. When he talks about God and satan, he takes on a preacher's tone and sounds as if he is excoriating himself.

Jerry Lee's life presents the spectacle of an artist, who, as he attains more and more mastery over his art, has less and less control over his life, demonstrating that art is one thing and life another and that they run parallel to each other rather than intersect. What should have been high points in his life have been disasters: his mother taken away before her time; two children dead; two wives dead—one under suspicious circumstances. For over thirty years, he has been wrecking cars, beating up his women, boozing steadily and noisily and popping pills by the bushel. It has left him with a tormenting sense of guilt and sin and a God he can placate only by giving up rock and roll, which neither he nor his public are prepared to do, in spite of his stating categorically, "There are millions on dope today who were influenced by rock, there are others who have gone off on every possible emotional trip. Had I known what I know now, I would never have played my first note on the piano."

Sometimes those nineteenth-century doctors knew what they were talking about. Said one, "The only radical treatment for dipsomania is religiomania." This is as true today as it was then and is why the most up-to-date drug and alcohol centers are spiritually oriented. "The sway of alcohol over mankind," another nineteenth-century doctor well knew, "is unquestionably due to its power to stimulate the mystical faculties of human nature."

"They call me the Killer," said Jerry Lee recently, "but

Jerry Lee Lewis. *(Credit: Anne Fishbein/Michael Ochs collection, 1989.)*

Jerry Lee never killed anybody but himself." But Jerry Lee is not killing himself. Drugs and alcohol are. In the 1980's, he had his gall bladder removed, and two emergency/intensive care operations have removed most of his stomach. Like so many of his contemporaries—his world-class peers in the music field—he has the disease of addiction. Unlike them, he has been unable to let himself be helped. He chooses to follow his own drum. "Well, you know he's a genius," says cousin Mickey cautiously, "and geniuses are touched with madness. As a child, I remember he always had to be right, no matter what about. It could be the least important thing in the world, but he had to be right." As Iago says (Jerry Lee briefly played him in a musical version of *Othello*), "I am what I am. Ask no more of me." This is probably as close to Jerry Lee as can be got.

Nevertheless, since the world knows his views only from his interviews with the press, it is necessary to point out that, in most of them, you can smell the booze coming off the page. An open bottle often finds its way into the text, and you can read him getting drunker and drunker. And when he charges (as he does) that journalists misquote him, one wonders if he can really remember what he said. And one wonders if this does not apply also to his state of consciousness when engaged in most of his anti-social acts. The way he communicates verbally is one thing. The way he communicates in his music is, of course, something else.

Perhaps Jerry Lee did make a Faustian pact with the devil, one that says, "The more dazzling your performance, the more cataclysmic your life." If so, that was quite a contract.

For today, as a performer, Jerry Lee, playing mostly in his original country and rockabilly style, can be matchless. No one had a more thorough command of the South's musical heritage. Continually touring the United States, England, Europe and Australia, on the road for at least 200 days per year, he has built up a vast repertoire and a loyal and appreciative public.

Recently celebrating his fifty-fourth birthday, reporters came upon a scene of domestic bliss at his home with Kerry, his wife of six years, and his newest child, three-year-old Jerry Lee Lewis III, bouncing on his knee and laughing as Jerry Lee played his piano.

Can it be that the devil did not take into consideration Jerry Lee's own demonic recuperative powers? He continues to confound. Perhaps Jerry Lee has actually outlived their contract; perhaps it has run out.

THE FERRIDAY THREE—
PART TWO
JIMMY SWAGGART

In October 1987, Jimmy Swaggart was caught with a prostitute outside a seedy motel in a notorious section of New Orleans. For one reason or another, his "shame" was not made public until five months later on February 18, 1988. During this time, he went right on preaching. Some of the sermons he preached during the interim, knowing the blow would fall at any moment, become in hindsight noteworthy. It is as if he were preparing himself and his followers for the coming catastrophe.

In one sermon in December, he emphasized that he was nothing but a poor, fallible, deeply flawed preacher. On December 20th, he departed sharply from his traditional Christmas sermon and gave instead an odd but impassioned one in which he identified himself throughout with Judas Iscariot.

Frequently during this five-month hiatus, as he had for quite a while before, he attacked the prevalence of pornography and blamed the United States Supreme Court for its lenient rulings on obscenity.

No man shouted more loudly than did Jimmy on this subject. It is a well-known fact that in his Bible College the students were made to peruse pornographic material to see just how nasty it is. This is rather like trying to deter students from doing cocaine by giving them a snort to see how nasty it is. The question that springs immediately to mind is: what if they like it?

Pornography was not the only thing that Jimmy inveighed against. In his book *Straight Answers to Tough Questions* can be seen his determination to control his disciples' daily behavior, as well as their spiritual behavior. Outlawed are oral sex and masturbation. Masturbation, he proclaims, is a kind of perversion: "For this act to be carried out, the mind has to dwell on sordid and filthy imagery." He comes down just as hard on dancing:

> It has been proved again and again to arouse lust and sexual passion. Even ballroom dancing, as men and women glide cheek to cheek, is harmful. Ballet classes and aerobic dancing are totally licentious. Even when dancing is not mixed, the bodily contortions are such as to arouse sexual passions in those that observe.

Here one is tempted to ask what about the jigs Jimmy dances so exuberantly when filled with the Holy Spirit and speaking in tongues during his sermons? Or for that matter, what about his beloved Aunt Irene Gilley, known for her lovely dances in celebration of the Lord? Surely they take inspiration from only the holiest of impulses and are dancing for joy.

In one of his sermons preached before the world learned of Jimmy Swaggart's fall from grace, he began dramatically: "Rahab was a harlot," he pronounced firmly. "Rahab was a harlot!" he repeated even more firmly. Then, pointing a finger directly at me, you and the camera, *"What are we?"*

But Rahab turns out to be an independent, brave, gold-hearted whore in Jericho who hides Joshua's messengers and helps them escape, for which the Lord forgives her her harlotry and transfers her to Israel to live happily ever after.

Jimmy ended the sermon by telling about a prostitute who
recently called him. In tears, she described how she watched
him in her motel room, put her arms around the television
set and was saved. The point of the whole exercise seemed
to be to show what decent, salvageable creatures are prostitutes. Or maybe he was signaling to his prostitute.

As no one knows better than Jimmy from his Bible, a
great many loose, seductive women—from all-occasion prostitutes to the higher-class courtesans—such as Delilah,
Bathsheba, Jezebel and Mary Magdalene, play a major part
in the downfall of Biblical heroes. The Bible positively
abounds with them. "The Bible," said Howard K. Smith two
months after Jimmy's fall, "has an enchantment with them.

"I think Jimmy Swaggart is an ephemeral phenomenon,"
Howard went on to say, "I don't think he'll last, though he's
certainly a part of something that's very widespread today.
It's in its declining phase now. I think [Swaggart's] sexual
drive must be very close to the surface when you hear him
attack it that bitterly. Powerful forces of human nature are
at work, and if you try to suppress the sexual aspect of life
by screaming at it, it's going to blow up on you."

Not just Jimmy but, over and over again, many religious
leaders have been knocked off their pedestals. Aimee Semple
MacPherson, evangelist extraordinaire of the 1920's, was
caught in a love nest. Madame Blavatsky, founder of the
theologically forward-thinking, all-embracing movement the-
osophy, was exposed for her bogus magic tricks, and one of
its leading figures, Charles Leadbeater, was accused of mo-
lesting young boys. Whiskey priests and failed priests feature
throughout the history of the Catholic church. In drama,
there are the evergreen prostitute Sadie Thompson and the
tragic Reverend Davidson in *Rain*. Religious zeal and sex, it
could be argued, produce the same emotion: ecstacy.

In his autobiography *To Cross a River*, Jimmy Swaggart
asked a veteran churchman where are the famous preachers
of thirty years ago. "There are not many men," he is told,
"who can stand blessing. They can't stand prosperity. They
can't stand fame. It goes to their head. They start to think
they are God. . . . and that's when they begin to decline."

Jimmy reacts by reassuring himself that the devil can't "sideline me with immorality, money or fame." The only way the devil could get there was to lead him into preaching false doctrine.

———

Although Ferridians clearly recall Jerry Lee as a bad boy who, when not being disruptive, was down in the school basement banging at the piano and Mickey because he was just adorable, they remember Jimmy only vaguely, if at all. They remember he was close to Jerry Lee and that, although Jerry Lee became a snappy dresser, Jimmy was sloppy and ill-kempt. They remember vaguely that he never gave his teachers any trouble, that he was an obedient child, though quick to cry, and that his rebellion expressed itself not with rage but with sulking.

Frankie Terrell contributes her lode of family lore. She feels Jimmy was "honest to God frightened to death" of his father, Son, who used to box. "Jimmy decided that he, too, would be a boxer, so Son put on the boxing gloves with him and knocked down Jimmy just as cold as the wind." Son Swaggart was very strict with Jimmy and his younger sister. They weren't allowed to drink Coca-Cola. "Oh, he didn't get to drink the Cokes and Orange Crushes that I did." Says Frankie, "Don't you know that made him feel different? You know the peer pressure must have been awful from his side of it. They were only allowed to drink Kool-Aid. It's cheaper. And then here's Jerry making all this money. He's got this brand-new car, and he slinks out of it at Jimmy's house and says, 'Let's go get a gal.' Clean white shirt on, money in his pocket, gold watch and rings, rings."

Frankie further reports that, as a youngster, Jimmy was conspicuously pure. "He never tried to look up the little girls' dresses, you know, like a normal boy. If anyone had a dirty book, he wouldn't look at it. He'd say, 'I forgive you,' but he wouldn't look at it. He wouldn't go to the Arcade movies. He said didn't I know it was an angel who used to break the projector?"

From the very beginning, Son and Minnie Bell were

Young Jimmy Swaggart: school days.
(*Credit: Roy Turner.*)

determined that he go into the family business of preaching. But in spite of early visions and his fascination with his grandmother Ada, when he reached puberty, he skulked away from the church, and when Son decided to become a full-time preacher, Jimmy experienced it as an intense embarrassment.

He found his release in the music that poured out of the black nightclub, Haney's Big House. Jimmy as an adolescent peered through a window of this nightclub just as often as did Jerry Lee. Perhaps one reason that Jerry Lee became so sensitive later on about his two cousins' "imitating" him was that he himself had so obviously copied his piano style from the black piano players at Haney's. Jane Huff, a schoolmate from the right side of town and star cornet player in the school band, also sneaked out at night to listen to the music at Haney's. Jimmy in both his preaching and his book tells a lot about himself. But one thing he doesn't tell is where he got his inimitable style. Is there a Haney's Big House that trains preachers?

At seventeen years old, Jimmy, an aimless, sloppy, unhappy boy who had quit school and spent most of his time in crap games, met pretty Frances Anderson, age fifteen, at his father's church in Wisner and soon married her. Neither family was thrilled, but slowly, Jimmy's future began to take shape. They lived in a trailer in Aunt Irene's front yard, and while Jimmy worked as a grease monkey for a Ferriday oil company, encouraged by Frances and an Assemblies of God Church in Natchez, he began to get back his faith.

Around 1958, when Jerry Lee was riding high, he generously offered Jimmy the opportunity to record a gospel album on his label, the famous Sun Records. After much prayer and soul searching—and with only two dollars and fifty cents in his pocket—Jimmy saw it as an offer from the devil and turned it down. That Frances stood by him was pretty remarkable for a girl in her teens watching the prospect, not even of wealth, but of living comfortably disappear. Later, looking back, Jimmy knew he was divinely inspired to turn down the offer because it probably would have led only to becoming part of a gospel quartet instead of a solo act.

His rise is the saga of an itinerant preacher traveling the tree-stump circuit to revivals around the countryside with a wife and a very small child. It was a saga of never being able to put down roots, of having to teach the child themselves and, later, having to yank him out of school in every town they stayed in for more than a few months.

Recognition came to Jimmy as it did to Jerry Lee and Mickey through music. Through the years, Jerry Lee had persistently offered Jimmy the use of the Sun studio complete with first-rate musicians. Finally, in 1962, two years after the death of his mother, Jimmy accepted. The gospel album he recorded there became successful. From then on he did many more, each one more successful than the last. It should be noted that it was Jimmy who did the singing, but it was Frances who insisted that the albums be sent to all the gospel radio stations. By 1969, Jimmy had a weekly radio program, and when the audience began to swell, in 1973, he broke into big-time religious television.

The more famous Jimmy got, the more it was left to Frances to control the expanding business side of their lives. Ambitious, protective, shrewd, always by his side—if not ahead of him—Frances easily became the most important person in his life, indispensable, ready to fight his battles, girlishly good-looking but a mother to him. She is not the power behind the throne: she has seen to it that, in the throne room of their kingdom, there are two thrones, his and hers. He is the wild-eyes genius. She is his energetic, ever-watchful custodian.

Penetrating their kingdom, journalists have found Frances very much in charge and running a tight ship. She likes her staff loyal, lean and busy, willing to take lie detector tests, to get weighed and to jog.

Says cousin Frankie, "They don't give Frances any credit, but he does. She decides where they sit and where they don't sit and what they eat. But this gal needs to be lifted up. She hasn't done anything wrong and she's cried so hard there's hardly anything left of her."

Perhaps most importantly, she has always given him emotional support by blaming Jimmy's misfortunes on satan. Early in his preaching, lodged in an icy-cold, drafty house in Chicago, plagued by fierce headaches and the blockage of his sinuses, he was ready to quit. Frances made him stay the course by pointing out that "This is just another trick of the devil. He's just trying to stop us. If we can hold on long enough, I believe God will show us the way." Even when their lives were endangered by a flash flood at a camp meeting—what other people would call an act of God—she assured Jimmy it was another act of satan.

Jimmy and Frances seemed to rise above all physical setbacks. But his recurrent coveting of Jerry Lee's expensive possessions was something he could not rise above. Whenever they were in the Memphis area, the Swaggarts used Jerry Lee's ranch-style house as a resting spot, even if their host wasn't at home. One afternoon at the home when Jerry Lee was away, Jimmy took off his shoes and silently padded through the house. In the den, he looked at the new recliner chair covered in green leather that Jerry Lee had told him cost $300. He stood looking at the chair, running his hand over its soft finish while gloomy thoughts filled his mind. The Swaggarts had never owned a house.

He and Frances began building their home modestly in Baton Rouge. This home grew into a two-million-dollar compound. Its grounds are bigger than those of the nearby

Louisiana State University. Jimmy's church there is the enormous octagonal Family Worship Center, which seats 7,500. It also contains Jimmy's Bible College, with one of the dormitories named Minnie Bell Swaggart in honor of his mother. There are buildings that house the staff and there are two buildings that house the Swaggart family. One is lived in by his son Donnie, also a preacher, his wife and Jimmy's three grandchildren. The grandchildren have a two-story tree house with air conditioning. In the main house live Jimmy and Frances. There is a swimming pool and there is also a high wall surrounding the property to protect the family from peering eyes.

At the height of his popularity in 1987, his ministry made about $150 million a year, ten million of which went to the Assemblies of God. He was on television in 145 countries. He had 564 missionaries and 2,000 syndicating radio and television stations. In building his kingdom, Jimmy became Baton Rouge's largest employer of unionized construction workers.

———

On February 12th, 13th and 14th of 1988, only three days before the airing of the scandal, Jimmy was preaching in Revolution Square in Managua, Nicaragua, to a spell-bound audience of 25,000. He was the first evangelist in Sandinista Nicaragua. Answering the altar call, 10,000 people came forward. Jimmy Swaggart had been invited personally by President Ortega, who was intent on proving his commitment to religious freedom. Americans of the far right disapproved of Swaggart's venture into Communist lands. But Jimmy had never played it safe. He got banned from Boston and Atlanta stations for stating categorically that neither Jews nor Catholics would get into heaven unless they were born again as fundamentalists. Jimmy in Nicaragua was in top form, his interpreter catching his fervor as he rendered his words into Spanish with gusto. Catholic bishops complained they were denied television time and called Swaggart a false prophet.

He announced he was off to the China mainland. "I love you, China! I love you, Japan! I love you, world!" he exclaimed. Being abroad always gave Jimmy a lift. A year before, at a stadium in Argentina, there had been a rush of people across the soccer field going to the altar in the grip of the Holy Spirit. The Argentinian newspapers called him a false prophet. Jimmy laughed. "This is what's fun about being a Pentecostal," he said. "the world already thinks you're crazy. The people on the block think you're dealing with half a deck, so you have nothing to lose."

And then on February 18th, the Jimmy Swaggart scandal broke. Debra Murphree, a sad, shopworn Delilah, was the name of the prostitute Jimmy had been caught with. *Penthouse* magazine, personally angry at Jimmy for his constant attacks on pornography and rock and roll, pruriently promised that in a coming issue, Debra would describe in graphic detail, with photos to illustrate, what Jimmy actually did with her during their trysts.

What he did was shocking only in its bathos. In the twenty or so times she saw him over two years (never for more than fifteen or twenty minutes), according to her, he asked her to assume sexually explicit positions, "like you see in the magazines." Then he talked dirty. And then he masturbated.

When *Penthouse* came out that July, it was an instant sellout. There was a certain hypocrisy about those who rushed to buy it, assuring themselves and others that their investigation was purely scientific, in order to arm themselves with suitable stones to cast at poor Jimmy. Absolutely no one admitted they were hoping to get turned on by what Jimmy got turned on to. For most, the sad sight of unlovely Debra didn't do it. Cousin Frankie Terrell wasn't curious. "They say she's got a hairy bottom. What do I want to look at a hairy bottom for?" she asks.

No matter how many x-rated minds are indulging in x-rated behavior today, they are still as unable to forgive a fellow sinner as they were in the last century. If there is one thing the public cannot stand about their idols, it is the discovery that they've been hoaxed. "There is sin—and there is a scandalous sin," explained Dr. James, a Presbyterian minister on a TV panel show around that time.

Jimmy's downfall proves a simple but hard-earned lesson. For some time during 1986 and 1987, he had been uneasily eyeing the undiminishing popularity of Reverend Jim Bakker and the fast-growing popularity of Reverend Marvin Gorman. And all the dammed-up feelings of envy he had about his rock star cousin, Jerry Lee, and, for that matter, his country star cousin, Mickey, seemed to burst, and a stream of rancor poured out of him at these two successful Assemblies of God televangelists. The real and fundamental rule Jimmy broke was the Golden Rule. He did not do unto others as he would have others do unto him. When he found out that those two evangelists were headed for sex scandals, Jimmy seized the chance and jumped in. It was largely due to the ferocity and persistence of his investigations that both of them were wiped off the air. Then the deposed Reverend Gorman, who lives in New Orleans, seized his chance and did unto Jimmy what Jimmy had done unto him. And he set his son, a policeman, to trap him through Debra Murphree.

A psychiatrist suggested that Jimmy strayed from the straight and narrow because subconsciously he was envious of Bakker and Gorman for having all the fun. In May of 1990, in his magazine *The Evangelist,* said Jimmy, "I realize that many people take great exception to my stand respecting the field of psychology. However, if one will bother to look at the book of Job, one will readily see psychology as it was practiced some 3,500 years ago. Its results then were no better than they are today." Psychiatry is one road that Jimmy will not explore. He is much more content thinking that satan did it rather than Freud.

The Louisiana Council of the Assemblies of God, in February of 1988, held a ten-hour session with Jimmy in which he apparently confessed his sins and his lifelong obsession with pornography. They ruled that he not preach for three months. But in the Springfield, Missouri, headquarters of the church, the elders were much harsher. They ruled that he was not to preach for at least one year, maybe two, during which time he would be disciplined and rehabilitated. Jimmy refused. Shortly thereafter, the Assemblies of God defrocked him.

On February 28th, Jimmy Swaggart preached at his Family Worship Center. Beforehand he had said, "I believe you will see a different Jimmy Swaggart." (Each of the cousins shares the quirk of referring to himself in the third person). "I have crawled to the foot of the cross to be broken and humbled and I say, 'Praise God, praise God, praise God.' I believe you will see a man with more compassion, more love and more understanding. The message won't be different, but the messenger will be changed."

Five thousand people were in the audience with uncounted others watching him on television as he confessed, "I have sinned," followed by cascades of tears. This sound bite was promptly beamed around the world. From his wife, he begged forgiveness. From his congregation, he begged forgiveness. From his church, whom he said he had hurt and embarrassed, he begged forgiveness. "To my fellow TV evangelists," he said, referring to Bakker and Gorman, "already bearing an almost intolerable burden, I have made your load heavier, and I have hurt you. Please forgive me."

He had asked himself many times why he had sinned: "I have asked myself that question 10,000 times through 10,000 tears. Maybe Jimmy Swaggart has tried to live his entire life as though he is not human. I think this is the reason I did not find the victory I sought, because I did not seek the help of my brothers and sisters in the Lord. David never blamed Bathsheba. He said, 'Lord, it is my fault, I have sinned. I have done this thing.' No excuses. No cop-out."

Then, obeying the Louisiana Council's edict, he did not preach for three months.

Commented cousin Mickey Gilley, "I'm really grateful that my mother is not here, because of what has happened to Jimmy and how much she loved him. But you have to admire a man to get up in front of the world to confess to the fact that he has a problem in a certain area."

Ferriday, under seige during the Swaggart scandal, had its funny moments as it played country bumpkin versus city slicker. Convinced that the answer lay in his hometown, the tabloids descended, their photographers staggering under the weight of their paraphernalia. They were looking for Jimmy's father, Son, to photograph. The local wits pointed them in the direction of a towering six-footer. They snapped. Subsequently, when his photo appeared in the *National Enquirer*, the six-footer stated he planned to sue. Not only was he not Jimmy's father, but he was born a year after Jimmy.

On May 26, 1988, getting into Baton Rouge to hear Jimmy Swaggart was a feat. A multitude of highways and skyways present themselves on the outskirts, and it is entirely possible, by taking one wrong turn, to end up at the precise place one started. A man observed once before fishing on a bank and then seen yet again in the same place twenty minutes later was finally asked for directions. He got into his pick-up, saying, "You'd better follow me." He knew the route very well, having been a devotee of Jimmy's. Even now, he was deciding whether to go in and hear him.

Inside the lofty Family Worship Center, the air ducts are pouring out a perfect climate of faintly scented air. The ceiling is cathedral height; the platform, a large apron stage; the auditorium has a rich red carpet and the seats are mauve. Up and down the aisles walk ushers in neat red blazers.

The people in the audience are well dressed, well coiffed, well shod. No longer, as in the past, are the Assemblies of God followers have-nots. Now they are middle-class haves. A friendly lady, who, if given a sanity test, would easily pass, inquires of a neighbor where she is from. Upon learning, she exclaims that it is the same state where her son has been living. Wryly, she adds, "I mean he was there but now he's come back to live with me again." She shakes her head. "That's the way with children today. They leave home and first thing you know, they turn around and you've got them on your hands again."

The program starts. The band plays. The choir sings.

Jimmy and Frances take their places on stage sitting on plain wooden chairs. She is the last word in southern chic, her every outfit an event. One day, you will see her in green eye shadow that matches her green jacket and her green shoes; the next, her dead black dress is set off with a bright lace collar. Large gold cluster earrings adorn her ears. Today, there are pearls around her throat, gold bracelets on her arms and a bouncy bouffant hairdo frames her face. And there is Jimmy in another one of his beautifully cut, custom-tailored suits, lined in red silk. He is shod in expensive, slender shoes. They have arrived in a new Lincoln. They own their own jet. The Assemblies of God have come a long way from Leona Sumrall in her simple white shift walking around Ferriday.

Now is as good a time as any to compare the three cousins' faces. They look nothing alike. They even look like different nationalities. Jerry Lee has a face like a tight fist, weathered and granite hard, American Gothic, like a dust bowl farmer ("I am Dutch, Indian and English," he has said, "that's a hell of a mixture." "We're half Jewish," says Frankie). Jimmy has Northern European features, German or Dutch perhaps, blunt, rounded features that show no strain behind them. Jimmy, who weekly breathes fire, has a face set in soft, gentle curves. From his high cheekbones, the corner of his eyes tilt gently upward. There are no anxious frown lines, knotted veins sticking out or neurotic twitches to show what he has been through. He is superbly balanced as he springs around the stage and, as a great many women agree, sexually magnetic. Mickey, who must watch his weight, is, feature by feature, the best looking of them. Possibly he owes his looks to his French Gilley ancestors.

Jimmy participates in the music, seated at a Baldwin piano. He sings and plays a nice song, rather Elvisly, "Look for Me for I will Be There, Too." Then he came forward and invited new members who have just joined his ministry to come down to the front of the stage. There are sixty-one of them, and when they gather, they are met by Jimmy and Frances, who shake hands with them. Frances is bandbox dainty from her pert features to her white silk blouse under her white bolero embroidered with black sequins, to her black silk skirt and her trim patent leather pumps. Afterward, when the Swaggarts go back to their seats, Frances pulls from her purse a dainty handkerchief, with which she daintily wipes her hands.

This was actually Jimmy Swaggart's second sermon after his public humbling. His first sermon, his *apologia*, went down well, on the whole, with a majority of people, but many journalists expressed dissatisfaction that he did not, so to speak, invade his own privacy.

He had promised us a vastly changed Jimmy, and early in the sermon, he delivers him. He tells his congregation that Christianity is not a religion, but a relationship between you and Jesus. It is a personal, private thing, he goes on to say, not conforming to a set of rules: "It is different with every individual. I would not have understood it a year ago . . . I've even learned, my brothers, that if you don't belong to my church, you can still have a relationship with Jesus. That's hard for a preacher to admit. It's not charismatic theory, but it's what I believe."

Jimmy begins telling the story of the death, the burial and the resurrection of Lazarus. Then, before you know it, he has connected it with his own troubles, but so effectively that you find yourself connecting it with your own troubles. The sermon is about prayers that do get answered, not in your time, but in God's time. Much is made of Jesus' tarrying two days while Lazarus is dying and arriving at Bethany only after he is dead. And then raising him. "The resurrection was not for Lazarus," shouts Jimmy, "but for the glory of God." Everything that happens to you is for the glory of God. "Though how in the world," he whispers, "can God get glory out of the wreckage I have made?"

An autodidact, Jimmy has spent much time with Greek and Biblical scholars and, in his sermons, shares what he has learned. Bethany, where Mary and Martha and Lazarus lived, he explains, means "house of the afflicted one" or "the house of undeveloped fruit." "This is a perfect description of us," Jimmy rolls on, "a perfect description of every single

Jimmy Swaggart. (*Credit: Star Times Morning Advocate/Guy Reynolds, Baton Rouge.*)

child of God." Later, he tells us what Jesus' groan sounded like. Said the Bible, He "groaned in the spirit and wept."

"The translators didn't do the best job there," Jimmy informs us, "as some of the Greek scholars here will attest to. 'Groan' in the literal translation means he 'snorted like an angry horse.' Jesus doesn't like to put us through this."

Jimmy works with five props: his Bible held aloft and flopping, the gold edgings on the pages catching the light and glistening; the microphone, which he hugs close to himself with one hand; his eyeglasses, which he pulls off and on; his white handkerchief, with which he mops his brow and which seems to grow larger each time he does; and the pulpit upstage, behind which he retreats only to drop a prop or two and set forth again prowling the stage. For this sermon, he adds another prop: a shoelace. Suddenly, in the midst of a fiery exhortation, he goes to the edge of the stage, asks one of the congregation to "hold the mike for me so I can preach while I tie my shoelace." Breathlessly, the audience watches as he ties his shoelace. Laurence Olivier would have applauded.

Like Shakespeare, Jimmy occasionally makes up a word when needed, such as "explanatorial," as in "I'm being very dramatically explanatorial." Like Shakespeare also, he casts away restraint when dishing up the ills of body and mind. There is no doubt that Jimmy's sermons are interesting, even apart from the pyrotechnics of his performance. His vividly told and vividly interpreted Bible stories give a sense of dimension within a spiritual or scriptural construct. In other words, they make you ponder different questions than whether you should wear the black or the red tonight or whether you should have used the niblick or the mashie for that shot or whatever trivia daily occupies the mind.

One question raised while listening to him is whether he really believes what he is saying. Suppose he's doing all this cynically. Suppose this show can't be run any way but cynically. Yet, might it not be just as valid to assume that sometime at the beginning of his calling, or sometime along the way, he really did believe in what he's doing? Suppose, in fact, you cannot run a show like this without believing it.

Suddenly, there is a moment of time in the middle of it all when the pyrotechnics stop and he seems to hit a bedrock of truth. He is describing himself in his den the night before last, watching the hours go by, unable to sleep, drowning in a sea of misfortunes, praying for God to answer him but getting no reply, struggling over and over with the disaster he brought on himself. Like Macbeth, he has supped full of horrors and his description of Frances, wan and weary, coming to him and saying, "Come back upstairs," resonates with Lady Macbeth's, "To bed, to bed. What's done cannot be undone." Anyone who has had a few black nights of the soul in the company of a bad conscience can relate to Jimmy as he goes on working his way through to catharsis. If nobody can get happy like Jimmy, nobody can unburden his heart like him. He has raised self-torment to a new art form.

So there is Jesus at Lazarus' grave, and here Jimmy inserts himself with Lazarus, as dead as Lazarus, right there in the grave, too. A stone fills the mouth of the grave, and Jesus says, "Roll away the stone!" To the casual listener not overly well-versed in scripture, it comes as a surprise that after the death, the burial and the resurrection the story is not over, for Lazarus could not roll away the stone himself, nor did Jesus. The people standing by, family and friends, had to do it. Nor could Lazarus, once out, take off his grave clothes, as he was tied hand and foot by them. Family and friends had to do that, too.

In the previous sermon, Jimmy's object was to apologize. In this one it was to thank those who accepted his apology:

> We need each other, do you hear me? I need you. And some of you can stand there and fuss and say Jimmy Swaggart deserves to be in that grave, but Jesus said, "Roll away the stone," and I want to thank every one of you on television. I want to thank you at the Family Worship Center, and I want to thank you in the choir for rolling it away. And I want to thank you for taking the grave clothes off as well as rolling away the stone. Thank you. Till you took them off, I couldn't preach. How many of you, like Jimmy Swaggart, need to die?

———

Afterward, upon meeting him, shaking his hand and being kissed, he seems, like all great performers, smaller than his stage presence. There are several Indians from New Delhi who pay their respects to Jimmy and tell him how much they like his sermon. Said one, "We come from an Assemblies of God Church in Delhi," and then he gave an embarrassed laugh and added, "I apologize."

"Not at all," said Jimmy expansively, moved, without doubt, by the Holy Spirit. "I love the Assemblies of God. I ought to. I gave them enough money."

———

Howard K. Smith's prophecy about the decline of the televangelists seems to have come true. A historian in Alabama estimates that the televangelist industry's overall revenues have shrunk by one-third. Jim Bakker is in jail. Jerry Falwell's staff has been cut from 2,000 to 1,500 and fewer stations carry his TV show. Oral Roberts has also cut his staff by one-fourth and has been mortgaging some of his ministry's 500-million-dollar assets. Three residences in California were unloaded for a quick four million.

Reverend Robert H. Schuller of the Crystal Cathedral ministry, considered by many the class act, stated bluntly on May 24, 1990, that he will end his television programs unless viewers send in some $3 million to cover debts. In an angry letter to a newspaper, one fed up member asked him why he didn't go ahead and discontinue his television programs and stop crying wolf.

Paul Crouch, founder of Trinity Broadcasting Network, has resigned from National Religious Broadcasters, citing lying and trumped-up charges against him.

Billy Graham, grand old man of evangelism, in May, 1990, asked about the telescandals, said: "The three areas that satan attacks God's servants on are sex, money and pride. I never put myself in a situation where I might be tempted. I never ride in a car alone with my secretary. If I am alone with her in my office, I always keep the door open. In any situation that I might be alone with some woman other than my family, I keep the door open."

As for Jimmy Swaggart, some 500 of his workers have been laid off. He has been dropped from two major religious networks, and his worldwide television coverage has been reduced to four or five countries. His missions have been closed down, and many students have deserted his Bible College. His ministers, in a quandary, are forced to choose between the Assemblies of God and him. The IRS is poring over his books, and Marvin Gorman is still determined to put him on trial for slander and libel.

Jimmy presses on, regardless. The year before last, he summered briefly in Jerusalem and baptized his two grandchildren, Gabriel and Matthew, in the river Jordan. More recently, he has been seen on television at a crusade in a town in Ohio. He is in top form. The voice is as urgent and emotional as ever, now a shivering whisper, now a glass-shattering shout, its every consonant given its full value and every vowel its proper place. His rhythm still mesmerizes, his timing and breath control are awesome, his accent Ferridian.

To one of his TV audiences he said, "The Lord told me when I was nine years old I would be called. You can say that call is abrogated, *but, honey, I know better.* What about those that kicked me? I'm trying to find their feet," says Jimmy, "so I can kiss them."

According to the well-known columnist Lewis Grizzard: "God may talk to Oral Roberts and move hurricanes around Pat Robertson, but I'll bet he tapes Jimmy Swaggart."

THE FERRIDAY THREE—
PART THREE
MICKEY GILLEY

Lightning not only struck twice in the same place in Ferriday, it struck three times. Last but not least came Mickey Gilley to take his belated place in the sun. He is the third spoke in the wheel, the spoke without which the story does not truly spin around. What astonishes is how all three cousins got to do what they most wanted to do and do it with a sizable portion of the world applauding.

———

Harrah's hotel is the gambling paradise of Reno. One-armed bandits seem to pursue you through the lobby, surround you at the reservation desk and go right up to the elevator. Will they be joining you in the bathroom of your hotel room, too?

Downstairs, in its plush Headliner Room, Mickey Gilley is performing. Enjoying his first show is a large table of teenagers drinking Coke and 7-Up and screaming rhythmically at the beginning and end of each number. They are still there at the second show, still screaming rhythmically.

148

"Why are you screaming?" they are asked between screams.

They exchange glances and one of them offers the obvious, "Because we like him."

"What do you particularly like about him?" they are particularly asked.

More exchanged glances. Then the same girl, presumably their spokesman, says after a thoughtful pause, "Because he's so real. Like, if you went up and talked to him, he'd be just as real as he is on stage." The others nod their agreement.

Mickey is real. And normal. And life-size. Especially as compared to his two cousins, who may be said to be larger-than-life.

On the stage tonight, he wears slim pants, cowboy boots, a dark jacket of some rich stuff and a very white open shirt with wide lapels, which set off his thick black hair and his finely chiseled features. A handsome man on stage, with presence, projection and a surprising touch of elegance.

Singing and playing the piano, he has on stage with him also a well-rehearsed backup of first-rate girl singers and well-picked instrumentalists.

It is said that Mickey has been held back, or pushed ahead, or, whatever, in performing by his stylistic resemblance to his cousin Jerry Lee. What has to be understood from the beginning is that they pursue widely different goals. Jerry Lee's way with a song is to bend it to his will. It is entirely personal. His aim is to get the audience to believe that the song is happening to him, often by inserting his name in strategic places, as in his gospel singing. Mickey, instead, submerges himself in the material. He becomes that particular man living through those particular emotions and, thus, takes you one step further into the reality of make-believe.

Though both men are consummate musicians, Mickey's touch is lighter, an iridescent shower of liquid notes, as opposed to the hail of bullets Jerry Lee fires at the audience. In short, Mickey's piano doesn't seem to take the beating Jerry Lee's does.

Mickey's licks and riffs and arpeggios are done with a touch that is titillating, tantalizing. His style is both sensitive and assured. He is essentially a honky-tonk romantic. Underneath his best numbers, there is always a delicate, almost enjoyable mood of melancholy, funk and booze. His voice, nevertheless, hits that searing, plaintive country note, that sorrowing country wail, with a deadly precision. Mickey is one of those country singers who release the melody full-blown rather than stomp on it.

There is a way in which Mickey's normalcy works for him. It is one thing to be in an audience and enjoy watching an extraordinary person, who neither looks nor acts like the average common man, perform feats of wonder. It is quite another experience, and a curiously comforting one, to watch a normal man doing something expertly that you cannot do at all but can imagine yourself doing. In this, Mickey excels. All normal men have to do, he seems to be saying, is raise their natural voices to make them sound like poetry. Of course, it only seems that way. Actually, it has taken Mickey at least twenty years to perfect that notion.

———

When the Swaggart scandal broke, Frankie wondered if she were going to have to "seek counseling for my sixteen-year-old and ten-year-old because they were jeered in school over it. Their uncle Jerry Lee had put them through quite a lot, but I had prepared them for his colorful attitudes. But this Jimmy thing hit us out of the blue. They used to watch him on TV every Sunday, and they cried over all the fuss and didn't understand it." It would be hard to imagine Frankie ever seeking counseling for her children over any scrape Mickey got into.

Three children, cousins of the same sex, born close together and growing up in physical proximity, doing the same things, attending the same school and the same church, often fall into the following roles: the eldest becomes the saint, the second, the black sheep and the third, the mascot. Mickey was the mascot, the one everyone hugged and petted,

Mickey Gilley: school days.
(Credit: Roy Turner.)

Mickey's mother, one of the Saints of the Assembly of God Church.
(Credit: Private collection Edna Gilley.)

Mickey's sister Edna Gilley, known as the Popcorn Girl. *(Credit Edna Gilley)*

Mickey's father Arthur Gilley. *(Credit: Private collection Edna Gilley.)*

possibly because he was so happily normal. Of the three of them, Ferriday liked young Mickey the best.

He was helped in his mascot role by actually being the youngest and by knowing all through his childhood the bliss of the unconditional love and devotion of his mother, Irene, and his sister Edna, twelve years his senior. Said Edna, "I thought I'd be jealous of him when he was born. After all, I had always been the baby, but I just loved him. I still do. I just adore him. I love him not because he's my brother, but I think he's one of the greatest people." Says Mickey, "I was a mother's boy. I missed the first year of school because I didn't want to leave Mama. If something had happened to my mother when I was a kid, there's no telling what would have happened to me. She was the only person in my life. I was spoiled rotten. My mother did everything for me. I came along at the change of life for her and so I think she probably paid more attention to me than she did the three others. Mother was very strong. It was like a lioness and her cub. I always felt together as long as she was there."

From the overloving mother, Edna gives us a glimpse of the overdemanding child. "I'm telling you that kid, he was after Mama. He wouldn't let her get out of his sight. And if he'd come home from school and didn't see her in the house, he'd scream the place down."

Irene was a fine woman, as every one who knew her in Ferriday attests, but for a long time, her life with her roving husband was deeply unhappy. Said Edna, after the famous incident when Irene was provoked to break all the windows in their Mercury, Irene prayed daily, "God, you've got to give me grace. If you want me to stay with this man, you've got to give me the grace to stand it." Eventually, says Edna, "everything changed because Daddy got high blood pressure and was real sick."

From the beginning, it would seem Mickey either wanted to avoid being—or was not allowed by his cousins to be—sucked into the whirlpool of competition they so relished. Blood may have played some part in this, too. His mother was not a sister to Jimmy's and Jerry Lee's mothers. The connection was that she was a sister to Jerry Lee's father, Elmo.

Wealthy Lee Calhoun was no kin to Mickey and, thereby, Mickey avoided another area of competition for his favors.

It may also be that Mickey's French Gilley ancestry played a role in setting him apart. Perhaps that vaunted French skepticism and love of logic have a part in his temperament. "Later, when I began to think for myself," is a way Mickey often begins a sentence to explain why he rejected the Assembly of God and did not become, as his mother fondly hoped, her "little preacher."

The Gilleys boast a family tree that goes back many generations and is written up and authenticated in a book privately printed and distributed to the descendants. His great-great-grandfather, Joseph Antoine Gilley of Marseilles, was a pharmacist who was decorated by the king for distinguished services. Mickey's great-grandfather Jean Baptiste Hypolite, born 1809, died 1877, came to New Orleans on a ship called the *Susan*. He did well in commerce and was part of a prominent Catholic family owning land in Orleans Parish, Franklin Parish, Richland Parish and Ouachita Parish. Incredibly, he joined the Confederate army in 1862, when he was fifty-four, as a private. In 1863, Vicksburg fell and the Confederate army surrendered, except for him and some 900 other soldiers who refused to sign the oath of allegience. They were sent to a prison camp in Indiana and not released until the end of the war.

Mickey's grandfather was Jhatme Gilley, one of Jean Baptiste's many children. Jhatme followed his two brothers to Richland Parish to farm the land. There he fell in love with Molly Leopold, whom his brother Jules was courting at the time. In December 1870, Jhatme rode his horse to Molly's. She was fourteen years old. He talked her into eloping with him, but Molly had a strict Baptist background and was hesitant about lying about her age. Jhatme took a piece of paper and wrote "21" on it and placed it in her shoe, so that when the minister asked her age, she replied, "I'm standing over 21." Clever Jhatme, that may have been his finest hour. His wife and thirteen children farmed the acres in Richland, and through bad management, he lost them all. He bought from brother Jules a saloon called The Daisy, and this would seem to have had a strong impact on his son Arthur Filmore Gilley and his grandson Mickey Gilley, for both, at various times, would run nightclubs.

Mickey's father, in his time, ran several restaurants and a nightclub that Mickey remembers because it actually had a color bar—that is, a bar that ran down the middle of it that separated the blacks from the whites. But what most Ferridians remember is Arthur Gilley's taxi service. None of his enterprises made them rich. Of being poorer than the other children in school, Mickey says, "I didn't feel any different because I didn't have the amenities, but they looked at me differently."

Mickey Gilley, aged four, with his favorite cousin, Norma Jean Gilley, in the 1940's. (*Credit: Edna Gilley Mequet private collection.*)

Mickey played with Jerry Lee some, but finally chose as his special playmate another cousin of his, a double cousin on both the Lewis and Gilley sides, pretty Norma Jean Gilley. She lived just across the street and for most of his childhood, until he was fourteen, they fought and played together. Then, from Houston, came a young stranger, Geraldine Garrett, who entered school a grade ahead of Mickey. He fell hard. Her father had come to put in a sanitary sewer in Ferriday, and the construction lasted quite some time. "I guess you could say I got involved with my first love when I was fourteen. I didn't know anything. I didn't know what manhood was or what a woman was really all about, but I was just totally infatuated with her. When they moved on to another town, I just died, and when I found out she was dating somebody else, it was like my whole world came to an end. I finally convinced her to come back and see me, and when she did, we eloped and got married. I got married just a month before I was seventeen."

Jerry Lee, Jimmy and Mickey were all three to marry for the first time within months of each other. And each married a girl who attended the Assembly of God Church.

One would have expected Irene to react negatively when her last born and best beloved son told her that he had married Geraldine, whom he could not live without. But Edna says, "My mother loved him so much that anything he wanted was all right with her. And even though they were young, since they were both Assembly of God, everything was going to be okay." Mickey and his bride embarked on what would be for him a perilous journey, which was to last many rocky years and was to test his love of music to the utmost.

Mickey's talent for the piano was discovered by his mother when he was eleven or twelve. And her brother Elmo had to tell her about it. It seems quite out of character for Mickey to keep "the one person in his life" from such important knowledge. It suggests that Mickey, the toy, the plaything, the baby of the bunch, somehow felt unworthy to aspire to what Jerry Lee, the genius, and Jimmy, the golden gospeler, had conquered. He hid his light under a bushel, underrating himself—as he has probably done all his life.

Edna describes how their mother found out:

> The people in our family are big talkers. They were probably all in the kitchen drinking coffee, and Mamie and Minnie Bell were talking about how well their sons played piano. Mama must have said, "Well, Mickey can't play," and Elmo said, "Yes, he can, you come and listen." And he said, "Mickey, play the piano for your Mama." And he sat down and played. So then Mama went out to work at Gilley's Cafe to make money and she bought him a piano. But she bought it for him to play gospel music, and Mickey told me later that when Mama would be gone, he'd get in there and play boogie-woogie.

Mickey went to Houston with his bride, Geraldine, to work in construction for his father-in-law; he was unskilled labor. Which poses the question: if these cousins hadn't made it with their music, where would they be without it? Jimmy, before he became a preacher, was a grease monkey for an oil company, Mickey worked in construction and Jerry Lee sold Bibles.

Mickey worked very hard at a job he loathed. "I worked as many hours as it took, as many hours as I could get in. I never shunned work. I guess I didn't even think about Jerry Lee until 1956, when his first record "Crazy Arms" came out. I was excited to have someone in the family in show business. We had somebody that had made a record, who was from the same walk of life as Elvis Presley. When Elvis opened the doors, I felt like everybody—Johnny Cash, Carl Perkins and Roy Orbison, all these people—came through and there was Jerry Lee right there with them." About a year later, Jerry Lee came to Houston to play at Dement Stadium. Mickey went to the concert and, driving Jerry Lee to the airport, saw him pull out a roll of hundred-dollar bills. The next day, Mickey went out and cut a record.

Then began for him the list of labels that he made records for, each company assuring him that when the record came out, he'd be a star. Minor, Potomac, Lynn, Sabra, Princess labels were all going to help him make it. He recorded "Call Me Shortly" on the Dot label, which was a near hit. He once bought a whole new wardrobe because he was sure that when "Three's a Crowd" came out, he would be a hot act. He drove to Philadelphia to try to talk Dick Clark into letting him on his show, but didn't succeed. And that's the way it went. From nightclub stints in New Orleans and Biloxi and Mobile, he ended up in Ray's Lounge in Lake Charles, Louisiana. There, in that small club in 1959, Mickey felt he'd hit bottom. His marriage was in trouble. With three kids, he and his wife divorced.

Discouraged, Mickey went back to Houston, worked on construction again for six months, but the strong pull of music lured him back to clubs. He spent the next fourteen years in clubs around Houston, mainly from 1960 to 1970 at the Ranch House and the Nesadel. In the early 1960's, he married his present wife, Vivian. Slowly, gradually and by degrees, each year, Mickey became better established in Houston until he was a local star with a TV show and had a local hit, "Lonely Wine," and his name shone outside clubs in neon lights. His reaction to his slow climb into the limelight might be called a typical one: "I knew I was going to succeed because I worked so hard."

In 1970, into the Nesadel walked Sherwood Cryer, eccentric Texas millionaire, who for all occasions dressed like a janitor in overalls. He came back often. He was much taken by Mickey's act, and he was much taken with Mickey, too. From a lowly welder, Sherwood had risen to being a millionaire by playing his hunches. He had a string of nightclubs and wanted Mickey to go in with him on one of them. It was a place called Shelley's in suburban Pasadena, outside Houston. Mickey went over to see the place and laid it on the line for Sherwood. "If you're talking about this club here, forget it. I'm not interested. My act's too high class to work in a joint, and that's what this amounts to."

"What'll I do?" asked Sherwood eagerly.

"Get a bulldozer and clean this thing out, and we'll start over." And after that was done, Mickey said, "It's an acoustic nightmare. The sound bounces all over. It looks like an airplane hangar." Mickey made Sherwood drop the ceiling, put paneling on the walls and then gave Sherwood a whole string of instructions that he didn't for a moment think Sherwood would carry out. It added up to about $75,000 worth of improvements. Sherwood made them. Mickey was beginning to enjoy himself. "Let's call it Gilley's," he said, and they did, with every other sound tile on the ceiling stamped Gilley's as well. Then, Mickey asked for a good salary for himself and his band. Then he asked for a fifty percent ownership. He got it. When Gilley's was completed, it could advertise itself truthfully as the largest nightclub in the world. It could seat 4,000 people. Along with other civilities, it had 150 different pinball and video games, punching bags for the customers to let off steam on, rather than on each other, and the famous mechanical bull, which women loved riding and on which every male Texan felt compelled to test his *cojones*. A Texas judge discerningly characterized the people who went to Gilley's as "rootless, lonely, short of money and on the make." He should have added, "And their cry is heard forever throughout this land."

In the 1970's, Houston was in a spectacular oil boom, which carried with it a building boom. People arrived by the thousands to fill the jobs, and at night, they wanted to drink beer and have fun. There wasn't much to see or do in Houston. After watching the Houston Oilers, looking at the Astrodome and the oil wells, there was nothing left but Gilley's. By the hundreds they poured in. Mickey Gilley and his club rode a fifteen-year wave of success.

In Sherwood, Mickey felt he had found someone who believed in him and whom he could trust. And with his trust there grew a mutual affection. To Mickey, Sherwood was "the first man in the business who didn't bullshit me." They became as close as father and son, a relationship which, afterward, when they fell out, allowed each of them to denounce the other with, "And after all I've done for him!"

Mickey Gilley.
(*Credit: Mario
Casilli.*)

Mickey Gilley's first national success was "Room Full of
Roses," which made number one on the country charts.
Mickey can trace its fragile progress far enough back to make
it all look like happenstance. Millie Elrick, who took the
tickets at Gilley's and was Sherwood's girlfriend, asked
Mickey as a favor to record for her "She Called Me Baby,"
which he did. For the flip side, Mickey chose to do "Room
Full of Roses." What drew him to it is some deep romantic
recess in him that surfaces sometimes in his conversation,
as, for instance, in describing his sixteen-year-old self in
love, how he "just died when he found out she was dating
somebody else," and that it was "like his whole world came
to an end." It was an old song that he and Jerry Lee had

fooled around with back in Ferriday. Jerry hadn't liked it much. Mickey thought he was probably right. What happened then was what happened to Elvis's "Heartbreak Hotel," recorded to be the flip side of "I Was the One." Someone by mistake turned it over and, as a result, Elvis sang "Heartbreak Hotel" on TV instead of the A side. Neither A side was ever played, and "Room Full of Roses," a runaway hit in Houston, was finally distributed by Playboy Records to repeat its success nationwide. Mickey was on his way. Now when he phoned his mother in Ferriday, he always touched base by warning her, "Remember, if you don't like what I'm doing, don't pray against me. Pray for me to be a better person, but don't pray against me."

Leading Houston journalist, Bob Claypool, wrote of the effect "Roses" had on him when he first heard it, calling it "a surprisingly delicate, almost introverted thing full of deep yet suppressed emotion. It was the kind of strong, almost magical, experience you have when you hear a great record under the right circumstances."

A high point of his life, says Mickey, took place in Nashville, when one of Elvis's entourage came up to him and told him how much Elvis liked "Room Full of Roses" and how often he played it.

It is an eerie kind of song. If he sent a rose to his beloved every time she made him blue, the singer laments, she'd soon have a roomful of roses. Good, morbid country blues stuff, but startling in its reversal of the rose, symbol of love and celebration, used here as a symbol of pain and despair.

Many of Mickey's best country songs are based on the classic theme of *La Belle Dame sans Merci,* the heartless lady who holds her suitor forever in her thrall. Capricious, cruel, inciting and inflaming—once gained, she is forever lost. She ruins his life, yet he emerges as neither a nerd nor a wimp but is elevated through his suffering to dignity. In "She's Pulling Me Back Again," the lover begs his girl to protect him from the siren to whom he's irrevocably drawn. A good example of Mickey's feel for old barroom ballads, "The Window Above" presents a macabre setting: a bedroom from which the groom sings about watching his bride night after night making love to another man. Mickey has the audacity to take this barroom ballad seriously and the artistry to pull it off and save it from guffaws. In "You Don't Know Me," the lover realizes his lady can't be bothered to. In "Bring It on Home to Me," he promises her jewels and money. It is interesting that the country songs, underneath the booze, broads, bars and homesickness, are all pleading for mercy, even the delightful "Too Good to Stop Now," which extols the almost unbearable excitements of love.

"City Lights," a country classic, is one of Mickey's best-known records. In it, he displays all his strengths. His tender intensity is reminiscent in its intimacy of the great French *chanteurs*. He perfectly captures the country yokel's lonely yearnings and baffled whimsicalities as he wanders in lyric desolation from bar to bar drinking sherry wine, complaining ruefully, "I just can't say I love you to a street of city lights."

For 300 years, the South has been exporting its way of talking as the only acceptable way of singing American music (as the Beatles and Rolling Stones have demonstrated), in defiant rebellion to the way the rest of America talks and pronounces its words. Mickey sings in what Ferriday's Mayor, Glen McGlothin, calls "Concordia Redneck." This consists, among other things, of putting diphthongs into words no one else would dream of and, perversely, removing the slightest hint of a diphthong used in standard American speech. Hence with Mickey, "mind" turns into "mahnd," "time" into "tahm" and the "great state" of Louisiana into the "gret stet."

When people achieve national success as late as thirty-eight years old, which is what Mickey was, it takes them differently than if they have achieved it barely out of their teens. Their personalities are formed by then and don't change. They are, without doubt, a great deal happier than before, but they tend not to go off half-cocked. Fame doesn't assault them in the same way it does the others.

Mickey driving his pick-up truck before "Roses" was the same Mickey driving his pick-up truck after. Of course, he had his private plane—after all, the two other cousins had theirs—but Mickey actually flew his.

Mickey, like his other cousins, built himself a mansion. His is on twenty acres of land with a big swimming pool and jogging track and a house for his in-laws. It is still, however, in the blue-collar part of Pasadena, where he had his first house, and "the neighborhood will make it impossible to sell at more than half its value," says Mickey.

If you listen to Mickey, he will always give you a totally honest picture of what's going on with him. While Jimmy often talks to God, and Jerry Lee frequently reminds us how He has bestowed unlimited talent on him, Mickey makes a virtue of humility, so much so that it is hard to realize he is a headliner at all the gambling casinos in Reno, Tahoe, Las Vegas and Atlantic City. His vocabulary is full of such words as "hope to," "try to," "learn to" and "would like to." Mickey's modesty betrays him in almost every situation. "I am going," he says, "to Vegas this weekend to gamble a little and to catch all the shows. See if I can pick up some tips." Doesn't he know what an extraordinary thing he just said? It is what every headline performer does in Vegas, of course— but what the others would die rather than admit to.

"Every time I find a song I like," he will confess, "it doesn't do worth a darn. But if it's one I don't care for and somebody talks me into doing it, it does great. My taste in things has really gotten to the point where I don't really know what's good." Mother Irene and sister Edna have done their work well. Mickey radiates trust and doesn't lie.

He is the least sophisticated of the cousins. His three huge diamond rings, the large diamond initials he wears around his neck and on his belt buckle are still a source of pride and joy to him. Jimmy may surround himself with Greek scholars, but no one in Mickey's circle has familiarized him with the names of certain film categories. Hence, when a movie director confides that what he really enjoys making is "black" comedy, Mickey simply asks, "Why don't you bring back Amos 'n' Andy?"

In 1978, fate decreed that it had fooled around with Mickey long enough and decided to throw a whole bunch of roses at him—roses in the accepted meaning of the word. The movie *Urban Cowboy* grew out of a 1978 *Esquire* article of Aaron Latham's written at the instigation of editor Clay Felker. Clay went to Houston and people took him to Gilley's. What he saw amazed him. Clay is very quick at diagnosing society; he picks up on trends and hidden themes; he has a nose for subcultures. The article went on to become the movie *Urban Cowboy,* with its contemporary statement that, although some Americans may have turned to God and others to gurus, more and more young Americans working in oil fields or construction have turned to the cowboy hat.

Much of the movie was set in Gilley's, featuring Mickey and his band. *Urban Cowboy* struck a chord that vibrated throughout America. Ralph Lauren based his collection on it and people took to referring seriously to "Texas chic."

Mickey, with his hit records, had become a star before *Urban Cowboy,* but, without doubt, it gave him a special lift. As Mickey described it, "From 1974 to 1985, I was on a party. It was like a dream." A working dream would be a better description, for he conscientiously touched all of his bases, showing up where he was supposed to in the expanding world of his success. He had seventeen number-one records, six of which, between 1980 and 1982, hit the top of the country charts consecutively. He had seventeen other hits in the top ten. From *Urban Cowboy,* he had two hits that broke the national chart records by holding simultaneous positions. He won two Grammy Awards, including the award for the best new male singer. He collected trophies from *Record World, Billboard, Cash Box* and *Music City News.* He has sung on TV with Ray Charles, hosted nationally televised telethons for arthritis and, from the Hollywood Chamber of Commerce, was given a star on the world-famous Hollywood Walk of Fame.

When the party was over, which it pretty much was by the mid-1980's, his wife, Vivian, woke him up and called his attention to what was going on with his partner, Sherwood Cryer. Vivian, an attractive, well-organized woman, basically runs Mickey's business. She handles the payroll; she is the controller of his company; she organizes his fan club. Vivian

was purchasing the majority of the memorabilia for the club
to sell and pointed out to Mickey that they were not receiving
the money that was coming to them; for example, either
981,000 T-shirts were missing or the money was. The time
had come, she told him, to ask Sherwood to see the club's
books every week. Sherwood tossed this aside by asking
Mickey how much money he needed, saying he would be glad
to give him any amount. It came down to Mickey's hiring a
certified public accountant, and what was discovered was
seventeen million dollars unaccounted for.

Meanwhile, Mickey took a good look at the place. Slipping into the cousinly third person, he described what he
saw as "very devastating to Mickey Gilley to see a building
with Gilley's name on it that looks like an outdoor toilet.
That doesn't project Mickey Gilley as the type of country act
that I represent in this business." The restrooms were a
disgrace, untiled, with urine running through the cracks
under the door. The parking lot was an obstacle course with
dangerous potholes all around. Moreover, claimed Mickey, it
had become a rip-off joint. If you walked into Gilley's with
ten dollars, Sherwood wanted nine dollars and eighty cents
of it. The dressing rooms were shabby. There would be one
price for tickets announced in the newspaper ads for the star
attractions, but the price would be higher when you got
there. When Mickey demanded these conditions righted,
Sherwood replied with his now characteristic answer: "Sue
me, man. Times are bad all over." By the end of the 1980's,
times were bad all over Houston. There was an oil bust and
a building bust. It was almost a ghost town with its myriad
see-through high rises.

The redoubtable Sherwood Cryer was considered a dangerous man to cross. Yet Mickey sued him in the summer of
1988 in a Houston courtroom. Said his manager, Sandy
Brokaw, just before the hostilities began, "What you've got
now is two guys just like *High Noon*. This is a western
allegory here. It might be a courtroom anywhere in America,
but it's in Houston, and they are going to walk out there,
and it might as well be the back lot of Paramount with Gary
Cooper and what's-his-name walking toward each other."

Sherwood, he added, had been like Nero. He fiddled while Rome burned.

Mickey won the case, the judge awarding him half of the missing seventeen million dollars, with the rider, "Collect if you can."

The court also allowed Gilley to remove his name from the building. Two years later, on the 4th of July, 1990, Gilley's burned down. It was thought to be arson.

Mickey's next rude awakening was when his record company CBS/Epic told him they were no longer interested in him. Remembering his hot-tempered father and his brother who was so pugnacious that if anybody hollered "fight" he'd jump in and say, "Where's it at?" Mickey very young had decided to be just the opposite. "I do anything I can to avoid getting into trouble."

But, like his cousins, he does get angry. "The angriest I've ever seen him," said Sandy, "was over his relationship with Sherwood. He just feels he went into this relationship with a lot of trust and good faith and that he'd been betrayed. With Mickey, it's just a raw anger that comes out. It's verbal. He doesn't really yell. It's just anger that comes out in his voice, and his face gets red, and his nostrils flare, and his eyes water. I'm impressed with it."

In Houston, if the radio stations didn't play his records quickly enough, he would blast them in the newspapers, saying, "They're letting me down. I'm Houston. They should be more supportive." CBS Records he blasted in the media. On a national country music program, he bad-mouthed his own club, Gilley's. Says Sandy:

My comment is he was rightfully angry at CBS, rightfully angry at radio, rightfully angry at Sherwood—but he has no diplomacy.

He really doesn't suffer, and he's not tormented.

He just likes playing his music, going around the country playing his music. As long as he can make a buck playing his music and play some golf and watch TV and have a beer, he's happy.

He's a real "people" person. That's his strength, but it's also his weakness. He's so easy with people. I've seen him talk to anybody, and that's great, but sometimes I wish that instead of spending time with those people, he could put that energy into meeting the people who can benefit him more. I'll be trying to get him to meet somebody and he'll be off talking to some drunk at a Howard Johnson's.

One of the first things Mickey did when he had enough money was to buy the house for his mother and father that she wanted the most. It was Norma Jean's mother's old house on Mississippi Avenue, just across from the house where Mickey originally lived. Furnished to Irene's heart's desire, the house is small but resplendent with chandeliers, brocade curtains and chairs, deep carpets, with astroturf on its porch. Irene and Arthur celebrated their fiftieth anniversary by getting remarried at the Assembly of God Church. Irene and Arthur, their marital storms abated, had a happy old age, Arthur dying in 1982 and Irene in 1985.

Sister Edna came from her home in Mandeville to Ferriday recently after attending a funeral in the area, determined to look again at her mother's last house. Even though her mother had been dead for four years, Edna was still not able to. Her eyes filled with tears as she talked about it.

"Every time Mickey saw me after mother died," says Edna, "he'd say, 'Sister, have you ever learned to make biscuits like Mama made?' Finally, I said, 'I've got to learn to make biscuits for Mickey.' I got it down good enough to call him and tell him to come and visit me so I can make them for him. So he drove all the way down just for two hours and I made them and he drove back." Is this a Louisiana French gentleman indulging his palate or a child longing for his mother?

In 1988, Mickey was left without Gilley's, which in happier days, he had regarded as his second home. He is in demand on the casino circuit, so he probably doesn't need a permanent forum. But as he said once, reacting to a slur of Jerry Lee's, "Jerry Lee [doesn't] love music any more than I do and one thing I got him beat on, I admire and love people more."

Where to put his love of music and people? Branson, in Missouri, in Ozark Mountain country, near Oklahoma and Arkansas. It is a beauty spot with a theme park that calls itself "the live country music capital of the world." There are twenty-two theaters. One of them is Mickey Gilley's Family Theater.

Sandy Brokaw sums up his twenty-year association with Mickey: "I've just had a ball working with him. I've gotten to go places, do things, see things that are just phenomenal. I've built my career and learned the business by working with him. It has been a great thrill to watch him grow from a struggling honky-tonk player and me begging to get him on different shows to Mickey singing on the south lawn at the White House. It's been a thrill."

PEEWEE WHITTAKER

When it was decided in May of 1981 to hold the North Louisiana Folklife Conference, sponsored by the Folklife Society of Louisiana, in Ferriday, Professor Pete Gregory, one of its coordinators, asked his Chinese American friend Jim Lee from Ferriday if there were any black blues bands in the area. Jim mentioned the highly-thought-of Hezekiah Early's three-piece band, and they were invited to partici- pate. It was a great surprise to Pete to find out that one of the musicians lived in his own hometown, Ferriday, and has for over thirty-five years. His name is Leon "Peewee" Whit- taker, a weathered leprechaun of a man, who says right off, "I am the oldest trombone player living and the best. I am ninety-two and three weeks old." (There is, apparently, some evidence that he is only in his eighties). Says Pete, "His name sounded familiar, though I couldn't place it. But he is well known in blues circles. For instance, if you go to London and talk about blues players, he gets mentioned."

Peewee's story is the whole history of black musicians in the twentieth century. He is one of Ferriday's jewels, an

Peewee Whittaker.
(*Credit: Peewee
Whittaker private
collection.*)

invaluable treasure, a remarkable musician who, through his
long and varied life, succumbed neither to drink, nor drugs,
nor to the church—a progression not that unusual.

It was Peewee's band that played at Haney's Big House on
South Fourth Street in the 1950's when Will Haney's large
house was filled to the brim every weekend with people
spilling out into the street, singing and dancing, drinking,
fighting and loving to the sounds of the best black music of
the day, played loud enough for everyone in Ferriday to hear.
Haney's was a home away from home for such musicians as
B. B. King, Bobby "Blue" Bland, Little Milton, Junior
Parker, Muddy Waters, Memphis Slim, Joe Hinton, Ray
Charles and Fats Domino, where they could all expect large
and enthusiastic audiences. For all these greats, not more
than youngsters at the time, Peewee and his band played
backup.

Up until 1967, when it burned down, there was nothing like Haney's anywhere around that part of the country, including Natchez, for Natchez had an irascible sheriff who upped the cost of dancing licenses for the black clubs until it became too expensive for their owners to operate. No such ordinance hindered the wide-open, ever-accommodating gambling and entertainment town of Ferriday.

Around 1954, a nineteen-year-old white boy, who as a young child had stood outside peering into Haney's window, now boldly came in. Says Peewee:

> The way I got to play with Jerry Lee Lewis, he'd come in and sit with us. He had ideas, wanted to make records. He'd ask for ideas and I'd show him. I showed him how to stop and take his time and all like that. He'd be with us every weekend, every Saturday night, come and sit in. They wouldn't allow him to play with colored, but he could sit in and play. He was wonderful around here.

In this black nightclub, Jerry Lee was not just playing with any old blues musicians, he was sitting in with the best. Peewee also remembers the adolescent Jerry Lee's picking cotton by pulling up the plant stalks and his father's giving him hell for it.

———

Peewee was born early in this century outside of Newellton, a town forty miles north of Ferriday. He was an only child, whose parents separated when he was young. He remembers his mother, Kizzie, playing guitar and singing blues a lot. When Peewee was a small schoolboy, a Professor Smith from Alcorn State, one of the oldest universities in Mississippi, would cross the river two or three times a week to give the schoolchildren musical instruction. It was not unusual at that time for black children to be taught to play an instrument and to read music. Nor was it unusual to do so even further back in W. C. Handy's time, as his autobiography attests. Peewee learned to play clarinet, trombone, guitar, bass and mandolin. Professor Smith, according to Peewee, was a strict taskmaster. "There wasn't much faking then. If you were learning music in school, they wouldn't let you fake nothing. Couldn't do nothing but read."

After fifth grade, Peewee and his mother moved to Lake Village, Arkansas, and there his mother gave up singing blues and became a missionary Baptist minister. It was there, too, that he became friendly with a schoolmate, Louis Jordan, the saxophonist, whose raunchy, exuberant band, The Tympany Five, was to enjoy wide popularity. Jordan's birthdate is given as 1908, which would suggest that Peewee's could be around that date, too. Jordan's father had a small band and was also a music teacher for the schoolchildren.

Seventh grade found Peewee and Jordan in the kind of high spirits that no school could contain. Says Peewee:

After I got up in music, my mama couldn't keep me in school. Especially a minstrel band, if they had a bunch of girls. She'd look for me and I'd be gone. Me and Louis Jordan used to make parades with nothing but me and Louis, us kids. I was on trombone and Louis was on saxophone.

F. S. Wolcott, the white man who ran the Rabbit's Foot Minstrels, came to town and was amused by these two rambunctious children. He put them in his car and every time they came across a parade, he'd plop them down in front of it. Says Peewee:

Everybody that seen me wanted me 'cause at that time it was a sight to see a kid or a girl or a woman playing in the band. Nowadays, they don't pay attention to that because the world done got full of musicians.

Around 1916, another family move put mother and son in Greenville, Mississippi. In 1919, Peewee began his long professional musical journey, where every place is home because no place is. He joined Tullus Washington and his fourteen-piece band. A large and prestigious dance band like Washington's would not consider giving you a job if you could not read music. Washington himself played trombone, and Peewee so admired him that he then and there made trombone his own instrument. The band played at both white and black dances, traveling within that magic triangle known as America's musically creative heartland that went from Alexandria, Louisiana, up to El Dorado, Arkansas, and down to the Louisiana and Mississippi Delta.

Around 1925, Washington and his band made a significant move which followed the pattern set down by many New Orleans jazz men: they moved to Chicago. Peewee did not go with them. Instead, he returned to Greenville, and in 1927, when Harry Walker's band came to town needing a trombone player, he joined up. For Harry Walker's band, you not only had to read music, but double on another instrument and sometimes play a third. Peewee qualified.

Walker's band traveled the same prestigious circuit as Washington's. No honky-tonks for them, they played dance halls and school and college proms, for both black and white audiences. Since neither Walker's band nor Washington's made any recordings, the only knowledge we have of them and their music is from oral historians like Peewee.

Quite suddenly, after eight years, Peewee left the band flat. He hitched and hoboed to Monroe in order to join the tour of F. S. Wolcott's Rabbit's Foot Minstrels. What impulse drove him to change course so abruptly, to give up the status of playing in Walker's band for the rough-and-tumble of a minstrel show? For Peewee, the answer was simple:

> At that time, anybody would hire me because I was a pretty good player, but mostly I followed them girls at that time. If I saw a girl on a show I liked, I'd leave just to get over to where them girls were.

Girls, girls, with Peewee hot on their trail, became a strong leitmotiv running through his life. Good as his word, he followed the girls from minstrel shows to circuses to carnival bands and back again.

Work was seasonal, with engagements primarily during the summer months. Peewee looks back with nostalgia on the winters he spent on F. S. Wolcott's large house in Port Gibson. He paints a picture of a sort of musicians' winter paradise, making his sojourns there seem like some glorious house party that went on for months. "When winter time come, I have eased around there . . ." says Peewee tapping a poetic vein:

> Mr. Wolcott was over there in Port Gibson. In the winter time when it get bad, we'd go out on his plantation. He had a big house out there for performers. For some, there was a railroad car on the land that had berths for you to sleep in. If you didn't have nowhere to go or nowhere to eat or sleep, or if you just come through there and were a performer or musician, you could get into that big place. You could get three meals a day and three tickets a week to the picture show and sleep there all winter. When winter time come, I have eased around there. I'd go there to eat and sleep over the winter. When it started to get warm again, I'd sneak off, go to where I done wanted to go. But I done made the winter.

Not all the white men who ran minstrel shows had the benevolent paternalistic ways of Wolcott. There were exploitive bosses. At one point, Peewee and Louis Jordan were playing for a "Mr. Charlie" at a club in El Dorado, Arkansas. According to Peewee, "This mean man would beat you to death if he wanted you to play and you quit. One Sunday, Louis Jordan went out to the bathroom. Never did see him no more. He done gone up north. At that time, you had to run away from them same as you killed a man." Or were a runaway slave.

White men at white dances could be just as aggravating. The band would start packing up, ready to leave, and white men would approach the stand with, "Woo, nigger, you can't stop playing now. My feets done just gone light. Come on, nigger, hit that thing." Says Peewee, "You had to hit it or he'd hit you upside the head with something."

For fifteen years, Peewee went from show to show. He would get nine dollars a week, which included room and board, and with this, he managed to marry, to buy a car and to raise four of his children to become school teachers.

> I'd ride my car all over the world. Bought me a new Ford and went from minstrel show to the circus to carnival

bands. That's all I done in my life. Never worked. I raised
four school teachers and never had a lick of work in my
life. Just playing music.

Peewee has been a working musician for over seventy
years. He is one of those lucky artists who are specially
blessed. What other people call work, he calls play.

In 1950, awaiting the arrival of the Ringling Brothers
Circus in Macon, Georgia, he stayed at the same hotel as
soul singer James Brown and presents this thumbnail sketch
of him.

They didn't count him at the time. They didn't trust him.
And he never could play straight music, you know. He's
the father of that bump-de-bump, you know, what they do
now, disco. He never could sing. But he'd holler and the
youngsters liked that. That's what made him so famous.
They didn't like natural music. He tried to prize fight. He
done swole his face up many times. I seen guys knock him
out and pour water on him. He hadn't made no records at
the time.

The ability to read music was important to playing all the
dance and minstrel bands, but for a circus band, it was life
or death. Peewee gives this eye-opening explanation:

You had to read because them [trapeze artists] were jumping by music. If you stopped on the wrong time and he
makes that jump on the wrong time, somebody's going to
get hurt or killed because they're going by the music. You
had to look out for your music at that time. If he missed
flipping or they missed catching, it had to be because you
done made your stops wrong.

In the late 1940's, Peewee formed a band in El Dorado,
Arkansas, and booked it with a chain of twenty-eight black
movie theaters owned by Sam Dorsey. These movie houses
presented variety acts long after the white movie houses
dropped them. One of the acts on the same circuit as
Peewee's band was comedian and film star Stepin Fetchit. He
was a quite different person from the frightened character

he played. He was the first black actor to get featured billing. He made two million dollars during the 1930's and squandered it leading the lavish life of a star. At one time, he owned sixteen cars, including a pink Rolls Royce. In the 1960's, he converted to the Muslim faith and was a close friend of Muhammad Ali.

Fetchit invited Peewee back to California to make some records. Says Peewee, "I got as far as Lake Charles. That's where I turned around." Obviously, Peewee preferred the girls on his own turf.

At one point, Peewee went back again to the Rabbit's Foot Minstrels, now led by the gifted New Orleans trumpet player, Dave Bartholomew, who would soon attain fame and fortune as Fats Domino's arranger. Around 1949, Peewee and Bartholomew played in the last performance of the last Rabbit's Foot Minstrel show. It ended its life just outside of Monroe.

About this time, Peewee had been looking for some place to settle down while, at the same time, continuing to play his music. And there before him, as if he'd rubbed Aladdin's lamp and made a wish, was the town of Ferriday. South Fourth Street was lined with juke joints. People came from miles around to have a good time there and, better yet, Ferriday itself had a very large proportion of blacks. But best of all, says Peewee, "To tell the truth, the girls in this town were so fast, and I liked that." Where the girls were was where the action was, and the epicenter of that action was Haney's.

Was Haney's filling a need or creating it? Did black Ferriday make Haney's Big House or did Haney's make black Ferriday?

Peewee and the musicians from his band settled down in Ferriday and were promptly hired by Haney to be the house band. They even hired a vocalist called Little Queenie.

For Peewee, there was the added bonus of Miss Mildred, a white lady who ran the local radio station. Miss Mildred quickly recognized Peewee's worth and soon became his friend, his booking agent and his guardian angel. Soon he and his band were playing regularly on the radio and, in the summer months, she booked Peewee as the only black musician with Doc Morris's band that traveled all over the North, Canada and even England. Peewee's experience with them was a happy one. "All musicians is musicians," says Peewee, "white or black. They together regardless. I don't care how long back, how far back. If you was a musician, regardless if you black as midnight or white as twelve o'clock in the day, they always count on one and other. Always did."

Nevertheless, after several summers of touring with them, Peewee decided to stay in Ferriday.

Big changes were happening in music starting in the mid-fifties and going right on to the mid-seventies, changes that would affect all musicians, black or white. Touring stars could no longer afford to travel with their musicians. That was fine with Peewee, for as the leader of Haney's house band, he was kept busy backing these stars.

Small combos were now in fashion, such as those who played with Fats Domino or James Brown. Moreover, musical "illiterates" were now in vogue. They were what Peewee called "bump-de-bumps," his perfect word to describe the sounds non-reading musicians made as they bumped off each other. The sound of James Brown's bump-de-bump band became increasingly popular.

To Peewee, it presented a deep conflict. He had loved the tight, precise orchestrations of a reading band. Would he change his style? It seemed a step backward. This is a conflict that confronts all artists in whatever field who have reached a mellow maturity only to see the new wave rolling in and the fickle public's taste change. They have become out of fashion, old-fashioned. They know of only one way to survive. They can't lick 'em, so they join 'em. And it is curious that, as time goes on, it doesn't feel to them so much like selling out as learning a new skill.

In 1963, Peewee, in his sixties, who had never been out of work—that is out of play—decided never to be. He threw in his lot with a bump-de-bump musician from Natchez, Hezekiah Early, whose band he had sat in with from time to time at Haney's. Neither could have made a better choice. Hezekiah, though thirty years younger than Peewee, was another survivor. As the trio finally formed itself, it consisted of Hezekiah on harmonica and drums, James Baker on guitar and Peewee on trombone. Peewee accepted the fact that with Hezekiah's Houserockers he would have to play in the bump-de-bump manner, and evolve a style away from the big band background and section playing to laying lead lines and improvisation. He had taken the big step. He was saved.

Hezekiah was excited at getting Peewee, knowing how much class he would add to the trio. Says Hezekiah, "Audiences were real carried away with Peewee when he came in with us. It livened the band up a whole lot. And Peewee would always walk the floor, walk around the audiences and play. People liked that."

Then, in the mid-seventies, there was another musical revolution that many bands, even the smallest, did not survive. Discos became the rage, and nightclubs had disc jockeys instead of live musicians. Steady bookings for live bands were a thing of the past. Hezekiah, ever the go-getter, avoided the disco route, and instead, headed straight for the Natchez aristocracy, who still wanted their musicians live. A bond was forged between him and the formidable ladies of the Pilgrimage Garden Group of Natchez, who booked them for a couple of parties and liked them so well that when they had their annual ball, the Houserockers were there playing from 10:00 P.M. until 6:00 the next morning. More bookings followed. The Houserockers were engaged to play at picnics, pig roasts, barbeques and wedding receptions. Says Hezekiah, "Playing for whites in town at parties was the only thing that kept us going." Young black people, it would seem, were not interested in blues music. To them, it was reminiscent of the bad old days of subjugation and segregation.

Hezekiah likes to tell a cautionary tale about Elmore Williams, a friend of his, a blues player and singer, who never would change his style. He says, "Back seventeen or eighteen years ago, blues was popping. Then disco came in and Elmore stayed with blues where it got to where he couldn't draw a crowd. People just stopped fooling with him. He always kept his instrument, so every once in a while, somebody would want him and they would get him. But blues began to fade, and you've got to play some dance music because people always want to dance. Elmore, he stuck with the blues and never would change his style of music. I had a talk with him. I told him, 'Say, Elmore, what you should do, man, you should try to change your style of music and come on in there with this James Brown stuff. Give them something they can dance on and you'll find that your business will hold up.' He said that before he would change his style of playing, he would quit."

————

May 1981 found Hezekiah and the Houserockers with Peewee playing at the old Ferriday High School auditorium for the Louisiana Folklife gathering.

Among Pete Gregory's friends and colleagues was Professor David Evans and his wife. He is Professor of Music at Memphis State University and Director of the Graduate Program in Ethnomusicology. Evans has done field work with blues singers for over twenty years. David Evans and Pete Gregory were stunned by what they heard, finding the sound, as David Evans said, unique and fascinating. Evans goes on to tell how they liked them so much they decided to record them, which they did, first in Peewee's little shotgun house in Ferriday and then on stage in front of an enthusiastic audience at the larger Louisiana Folklife Festival in Natchitoches. They called the album that resulted *Since Ole Gabriel's Time* because Peewee, when asked how long the music on the album had been played, replied, "Since ole Gabriel's time." After that, Peewee was inducted into the Louisiana Folklife Hall of Master Folk Artists.

In his notes for their LP, David Evans has written the most comprehensive study of a Louisiana blues group ever undertaken.

Hezekiah and the Houserockers has an enormous repertoire that enables them to play for five to six hours without repeating a number. Says Professor Evans, "Their music draws upon the traditions of fife and drum, blues, ragtime, minstrelsy, jazz, country music, rock and roll, rhythm and blues and middle-of-the-road pop. In other words, it draws from virtually every kind of secular music that has been heard in their communities for the past 150 years. In a single evening, one might hear this group perform such diverse pieces as "I'm Going to Move to the Outskirts of Town," "St. Louis Blues," "Whole Lotta Shaking Going On," "Blues Stay Away from Me" and the "Peter Gunn Theme." Essentially, they are a blues band, and blues lie at the heart of the repertoire.

Their sound is utterly distinct, as how could it help but be, with trombone and harmonica playing together. Even their guitarist, James Baker, adds to the band's distinctiveness by tuning his instrument with the unusual "cross Spanish" tuning.

The intermingling of the haunting train sounds of Hezekiah's harmonica together with Peewee's bubbling, talking horn make the band sound classical and eternal without sounding embalmed.

They are, above all, a dance combo. Says Hezekiah, "We always stayed with something that people would dance on. You got to play the type of music people can dance off of." The band also has disco numbers. "Yeah, we got a few beats we can disco on," he says.

The LP the Louisiana Folklife Society recorded has become popular enough to be reissued. Take as an example of its bill of fare an original composition by Hezekiah, a dance number he calls "Soul Around Blues," which shows off Peewee's beguiling, horn-playing answers to Hezekiah's harmonica questions. Peewee's horn can growl or snarl or slide with innuendo. It can sigh with sadness. It can mock or sympathize. Its comment on the vocalist's words is both amused and amusing.

Though this trio plays together with seamless teamwork, each maintains an individuality appropriate to his age and attitude. Hezekiah wears a burnt orange jumpsuit, James Baker, the youngest, an embroidered ethnic overblouse and his hair in a modified Afro. Peewee is dapper in a dignified dark suit and light blue shirt with a colorful striped tie worn in a dashing Windsor knot.

After his success at the Louisiana Folklife Festival, Peewee's fame began to extend beyond his community. In 1982, the Houserockers played at the World's Fair in Knoxville, Tennessee. But in what was most certainly a high point in his career, in 1984 in New Orleans, Peewee and his musicians *opened the World's Fair.*

In 1986, Peewee and the Houserockers, accompanied by Professor Evans, who also plays guitar, made two European trips, each for several weeks. They played at cultural centers all over Europe. Angoulême, Reims, Compiegne and Marseilles in France. They went to jazz festivals in Spain and in Berlin. They played in clubs in Belgium and at the Amsterdam Blues Festival. They went on to çlubs in Florence and to the Folk Studio in Rome. After that, they did a quick tour around France again.

"Peewee on tour tended to be rather silent, taking an interest in everything around him but not commenting much," said David Evans. "Most of us got sick due to the grueling schedule of long drives and plane flights at odd hours, but he got through the tour in fine shape without any problems. He was very active on stage, doing tricks with his trombone and walking among the audience as he played. He made a great hit on both tours."

———

Peewee had always wanted a trailer for a home. With the money he made opening the New Orleans World's Fair, he was able to purchase one.

Driving through the black part of Ferriday out to Peewee's trailer, looking at the tumbledown shacks, the people of all ages so bright and fresh, so colorfully dressed, the youngsters running around, the grown-ups watching the passing scene, you can utterly lose your rationality in admiration of a poverty seeming so picturesque. Unfettered by truth, you judge their lives to seem so pleasant and carefree under the sun as to be enviable.

In Peewee's trailer, there is a small music box in the shape of a merry-go-round on a shelf, a souvenir, perhaps, of his circus or carnival days, on the stove, chicken is frying, nearby on a countertop is an ashtray decorated with a figurine

Peewee in his trailer home while his large screen TV plays "The
Price is Right." (*Credit: Rhett Powell.*)

of a sexy blond lady in a strapless evening dress lying prone.
On the wall hangs a print of Jesus. He is young and beardless.
A plaque on the wall says "Hall of Master Folk Artists,
Northwestern State University, Natchitoches, Louisiana,
and then Peewee's name. Framed on another wall is a joke
one-thousand-dollar bill. Sitting in his trailer, Peewee looks
trim and in good shape. On the large screen television the
picture is on—"The Price is Right"—but the sound is off.

Peewee is hospitable. Conversations with him often take
unexpected and thought-provoking turns. Asked how he liked
Europe on his last trip, he replied, "I like it. It's clean. They
don't have no trees there, so they don't have no 'skeeters' and
snakes. You can lay right out on the grass without being
bothered."

Did he like Rome? "Rome was a bad country, you know.
It hated Christianity worse than any other country. If you
was poor and didn't have no money, they had these lions
would eat you up. But you could pay your way out of it. It
was a bad country." What about England? "Next time I go
there, I'm going to stay with the Queen."

Peewee's wife comes back in and fixes the chicken. She

would seem to be too young to be his first wife and is probably the second. Adolescent boys drift in and out. Are any of them his? Sure, he says, they all are.

Today, when Peewee and the Houserockers play around Ferriday or Natchez, other musicians, hearing of the gig, ask to sit in. They are always received graciously. Some of them are even good. The band now plays not only to black or white audiences separately, but to mixed audiences at festivals around Louisiana. For Peewee, this is simply the latest phase in a remarkable career that bridges the gap from ragtime to rock, from swing to soul.

Today Peewee is semi-retired. He is content in Ferriday, yet something in him yearns for the romance of the road.

Peewee says it better:

The world don't owe me nothing now. I'm through with it. I can afford to sit down. Of course, it worries me in the summertime when I sit and think about it, or either some of these guys call me or write me where they're at, in Chicago and places, what times they're having, you know. "We're here. We'll be here for about six weeks. Boy, we're having a good time!" All that kind of stuff, it worries me sometimes. That's why I started working again. To keep that off my mind, you know. When you're working, you ain't got time to think.

12

FERRIDAY TODAY

I enter the town of Ferriday as dusk is falling, and I make out a group of senior citizens—farm people by the look of them—sitting in line on an old wooden bench in front of an old wooden frame house. Only when I am practically on top of these folk, do I realize they are life-size rag dolls for sale in the house behind them. Their embroidered faces on stocking heads bear an uncanny resemblance to southern archetypes.

I arrive at the Patricia Motel, where I will be staying. The TV in the lounge, as in motels all over the world, is playing "I Love Lucy" with the sound turned down low. "There is no restaurant here," says Needra White, the young woman behind the desk, "but Brocato's is down the road, and we have coffee twenty-four hours a day," which means, I discover, good conversation, as well, twenty-four hours a day, with Louisiana coffee that is strong, delicious and addicting.

Needra's had quite a day. She's had to rush her little five-year-old to the doctor. It seems the child wanted to put eye drops in her eyes like she'd seen her mother do, so she got

Even in the
daytime, these
rag dolls look
real. They are
made by
Mrs. Russ,
owner of the
Russ Flea
Market. (*Credit:
Jarrett Reeves.*)

ahold of a tube of Super Glue, put two drops in her eyes and they stuck together. The doctor reassured Needra it wouldn't do her child any harm and then, with a pair of scissors, cut off her eye lashes, so at last she could open her eyes and all was well. Looking back, I see this mishap as somehow a Ferriday mishap: endemic to Ferriday though to no other place in the world.

The next morning, I go to Louisiana Avenue, starting at First Street and walking up. I am told it is the center of town. But where is the center? Where is that quaint village green or village square with the gazebo or bandstand or war memorial in the middle? Where is the white framed court-house and the quaint little inn and the quaint little antique shops? A decade ago, Ferriday was described in a New Orleans newspaper as "a spiffy little town with a clear sense of civic pride in its Main Street, clean swept, brightened with pots of plants before its shops, which offer every conceivable necessity. It is sensible, efficient yet relaxed."

For the past five years Ferriday has been described as "faded," "ugly" and "finished" until as recently as January 1991, when its ·CPA, Myles Hopkins, triumphantly an-nounced its finances "the best in ten years." It is Marty Nathanson's view that the new hydroelectric plant, one of the largest in the world, just completed on the Mississippi south of Vidalia, will generate with its cheap power so much industrial employment in the area that Vidalia and Ferriday will eventually become one prosperous megalopolis.

But seen today, the landmarks I was looking forward to— Pasternacks and the Arcade Theatre—are long empty and soon to be demolished. However, we are not talking architec-tural marvels, we are talking people: colorful, unique, in-tensely human. Says one Ferridian, "We got a lot of good people here, we got a lot of rascals, too. But they can become good." The chance of salvation is never far away. With a population of about 5,000 people, there are twenty-seven churches, as well as almost daily meetings of AA, Al-Anon, ACA, NA and Parents Anonymous, all available in the vicinity.

Ferriday has other problems. The water supply has been

Today looking west on Louisiana Avenue. (*Credit: Rhett Powell.*)

worked on for two years, and for two years, it has still flowed out rust-colored (too much magnesium, they are assured, though drinking it is not a health problem). Garbage disposal has not been satisfactory. Their robberies have a contemporary ring to them: on the 4th of July, four men ganged together to break into a drugstore to steal several containers full of Valium. On the other hand, there is good news. As part of a farming community always dependent on the weather, after three disappointing harvests, this year, they had their best cotton crop ever.

Ferriday's biggest problem seems to be how to keep its elected officials on the straight and narrow. This year, both the sheriff, Hubert McGlothin, and the black former mayor, Sammy Davis, Jr., were investigated by the FBI. McGlothin plea bargained and resigned. A president of the police jury, the governing body, has stepped down while his finances are investigated for "alleged abuse of public money," according to the *Concordia Sentinel*. The town keeps its sense of humor: a T-shirt has been made saying "I survived Ferriday."

The chance of salvation is never far away. *(Credit: Rhett Powell.)*

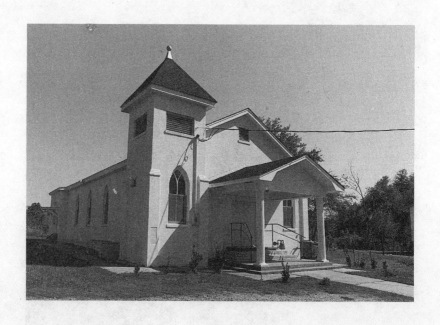

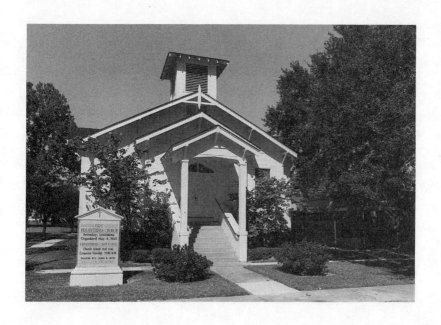

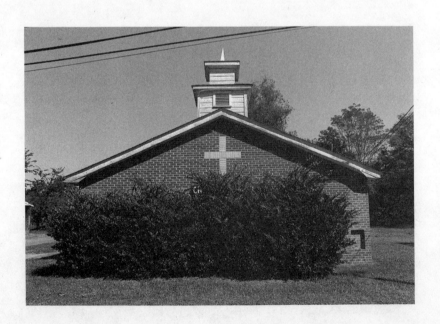

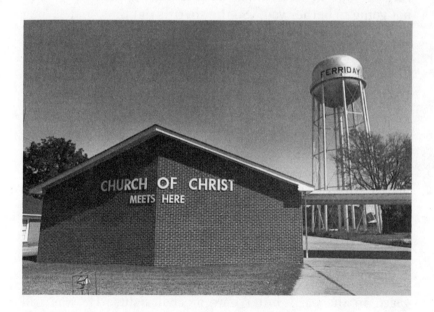

Sammy Davis, Jr. (his real name), was indicted by a grand jury on three counts of malfeasance and one count of injuring public records. Another charge against him, also reported in the *Concordia Sentinel,* is failure to pay IRS withholding taxes after they'd been withheld from paychecks of employees. The case is now in trial motion and ex-mayor Davis intends to contest the charges.

It is historian Joe Gray Taylor's view that corruption has been more or less institutionalized in Louisiana politics since the French colonial officials expected to get rich while governing. Institutional corruption exists in other states, but Louisianans seem more open in acknowledging it. Louisiana politics seem to operate under a different set of ethics than those of the rest of the country. Louisiana has always liked its politics piquant, as well as its sauces.

Says Richard Alwood, principal of Ferriday's elementary school and son of the late Lawrence Alwood of Delhi, "Historically, Concordia Parish didn't have money or ways to enforce the law. The message the officials got was, 'You take care of your little area and keep it halfway straight. We're not going to bother you.' So the sheriffs did that, and as long as things went on fairly smoothly, no one bothered them."

Sammy Davis, Jr., was Ferriday's first black mayor, 1984 to 1988. The black population was fifty-one percent at the time and they supported him. Extremely personable and well educated, he has an M.A. in English. Before he became a high-school principal, he successfully taught English at a Cajun school to children who had been expecting to be taught by the other Sammy Davis, Jr. During the segregation troubles in the 1960's, as principal in the Ferriday black high school, he was fired along with twenty-one other teachers (some white). They took the case to the Supreme Court and won it. It would be nice to be able to say in this imperfect world that Davis's tenure as mayor was an unqualified success, but that was not the case.

Mayor Davis was actively, honorably and militantly engaged in the early bitter days of civil rights. He was still militant in the late 1980's, when America liked its black

Richard Alwood, son of Lawrence Alwood, and principal of Ferriday's elementary school with students, left to right, Jamie Dawson and Reginald Bass. *(Credit: Rhett Powell.)*

Former mayor of Ferriday, 1980–1984, Sammy Davis, Jr., studying agenda at town meeting. *(Credit: Rhett Powell.)*

politicians healing and moderate like Governor Douglas Wilder of Virginia and Mayor David Dinkins of New York.

At the beginning of his term, Mayor Davis would enter a conference room holding a Thompson sub-machine gun, explaining that the city had bought it some years ago to "keep the blacks in this town in their places, never realizing that a black man might one day be mayor and the one to determine what's done with these." He was also a stern critic of Ferriday, calling it "a tombstone sort of place," when interviewed. After a carping article written by Mayor Davis in the *Natchez Democrat* in 1988, K. B. Watkins, a black businessman in Ferriday, a rancher, disabled veteran and vice-president of the Ferriday chapter of the NAACP, upset and angered by the racist tone of Davis's article, replied in a letter to the *Concordia Sentinel*. Paragraph by paragraph he refuted Davis's accusations, as, for instance, alleged Klan activity. Watkins found it strange that Mr. Mayor was the only one being harrassed by the Klan. He concluded the mayor would serve Ferriday better "if he spent more time and effort trying to unite all the people of the town and bring about better race relations instead of stirring up old memories that happened long before most of your eligible voters were born."

After being defeated in the mayoral election of 1988 by Glen McGlothin of the barbering family, ex-Mayor Davis was given a banquet in his honor by the Concerned Citizens of Ferriday at the Sheraton Hotel in Natchez. The dining room was at its most festive. On the center of each table were the largest magnolias in the world sprinkled with gold dust. The napkins were black and so were the match folders. One of the speakers noted that, although the banquet was well subscribed, the room was not filled. Looking around, I saw many more women than men. Said Davis when he got up to speak, referring to the election, "Ladies and gentlemen, I was robbed." He also said that until blacks got into politics, the word "accountability" was never used. He talked about the "weak giant syndrome," whereby blacks, although the ninth largest group of consumers in the world, are still using this power to make others rich. He joked about whites' unfairly high expectations of blacks. "They want you to walk on water. They want you to change the water to wine. And not drink it." He ended with a rallying cry: "We may be driven out. We may be kept out. But we won't be left out."

Meanwhile, Davis breeds and trains Rottweilers, a species of German police dogs. He tells me he is writing his autobiography. It will be called *Born in Injustice, But Not Prepared to Grow Old in It.*

———

After the banquet, I was standing in line to say hello to Steve Thompson, state senator for the district. The woman in front of me was saying crisply, "I voted for you, Senator. Now what are you going to do for me?" and expecting to be answered. Black women in Ferriday, I am told, don't fool around with "How are your lovely wife and children, Senator?" They get right to the point. If the church is the backbone of the black people, its head and shoulders are its women.

———

Mayor Davis was responsible for one thing that made a big difference to the town of Ferriday. He got a state subsidy for $300,000 to build a children's clothing plant that employs a force of 150, mostly black women, "and it didn't cost Ferriday a dime." It's called Kelly's Kids and is the inspiration of a young housewife named Lynn James, who didn't know how to sew, but knew how to design. Along with the Pasternacks, she is shining proof of what happens when you build a better mousetrap. No less than the nation has come to her door. What her children's clothes have that others don't, besides wonderful styles and materials for very little money, is that every garment is fully lined, which is unheard of, even in high-priced collections. For sale are pinafores, shirts, pullovers, overalls, sweatshirts and sweatpants, bubble suits for infants and jogging suits for adult women. Each child can choose from a dozen appliques, such as Winnie the Pooh (with a balloon). They are sold like Tupperware. All over the

At Kelly's Kids plant. (*Credit: Rhett Powell.*)

states, women gather for parties where the hostess, for a commission, displays the clothes. Kelly's Kids is so successful that it is opening up another plant in Jonesville.

Says Davis, "It brought work to black women, and that's a very big concern of mine because the majority of households are women-oriented. They're the ones who work steady. They're going to buy some food. They're going to send their children to school. But if the money isn't there, the kids will go to school angry and hungry. So my thing is to do whatever is necessary to get employment for women. The women keep the family together. In my case, I was raised by two grandmothers. I've been in the school business long enough to know the kids have to have food in their stomachs and wear some good clothing. It doesn't have to be very fancy. That's what it's going to take."

———

Ferriday has always been a town which takes pride in its athletes, white and black. Its black athletes have played with the Green Bay Packers and Miami Dolphins (Robert Barber),

the Houston Oilers (Walter Johnson) and the San Diego
Chargers (Mack Moore). Johnny Lloyd, who was one of the
original members of the Harlem Globetrotters, later played
pro baseball and, after that, was a high-school coach in
Ferriday. Last year, there emerged from Ferriday High School
the dynamic figure, the star of every basketball game he
played in his senior year, Shawn Griggs, six-feet six-inches,
195 pounds. At the end of his spectacular senior year he had
over sixty colleges courting him. He chose LSU, and sat out
his freshman year. This year, as a forward on its team, he is
already a man to be watched. His debut, said a Louisiana
newspaper, provided the game's exclamation point.

If you stay around Ferriday for any length of time, you
will notice that many of its politicians are barbers as well.

"Barbershops," says editor Sam Hanna, son of a barber,
"are spawning grounds for politicians. I know. I came up in
one, too. My dad, a barber, bought his shop from a man
named Ed Randall who moved to Winsboro from Ferriday.
You guessed it. He became the sheriff of Franklin Parish.
Not to mention Glen McGlothin and Hubert McGlothin of
the same barbering family, one becoming mayor of Ferriday
and the other sheriff of Concordia Parish. In Vidalia, one
police chief and one member of the police jury are barbers."
Every morning, Sam goes to four places. The post office, the
Concordia Bank, where the elders gather, a barbershop and
Brocato's Restaurant for breakfast. Says Sam, "Either I ask
them 'What's happening? What's new?' or they ask me."
Sam's lively paper, the *Concordia Sentinel,* won ten newspaper awards last year, which is about average for it to win
every year.

Dan Richey, a former state senator for the Ferriday
district, muses on the subject of political barbers: "This
phenomenon of barbers and politics is quite predominant in
our area. Barbers do more talking and listening and come
into more contact with other people than any other type of
job. On a weekly basis, a pharmacist or a realtor or a doctor
or a lawyer is only going to come in contact with the same
people. In the course of a week's time, a barber is going to

Early elders wait for the others at their regular morning meeting at the bank. (*Credit: Rhett Powell.*)

Brocato's restaurant: the regulars at breakfast. (*Credit: Rhett Powell.*)

come in contact with every type of worker in the entire parish, farmer, fisherman, you name it, if you have the gift of gab, like most barbers do."

This could pertain as well to the barber clergy, for barbers seem to become evangelical preachers, as well. The Reverend Huey Bradford, the Assembly of God preacher in Ferriday, is a barber, as is the preacher in Ridgecrest. Dipping far back, Lester Sumrall, Leona's illustrious brother, began as an itinerant barber.

Just after Glen McGlothin defeated Sammy Davis, Jr., and became mayor, I went to see Glen in his barbershop. He is in his forties and wore an incipient beard, he said, to balance his thinning hair. As Davis went through Korea, Mayor McGlothin went through Vietnam. He is a man who likes to get along with everyone. Says Glen, "I believe I'm the talkingest barber that ever lived. Here in the shop, we talk about anything from government to why we need rain to who's planting right to who won the ball game. We go from

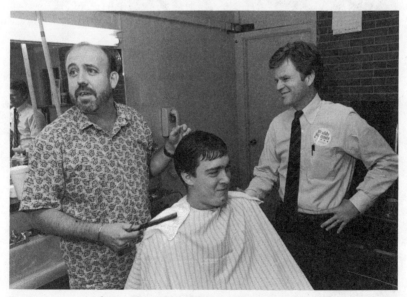

Present mayor of Ferriday, Glen McGlothlin, in his barbershop, left, with customer and Governor of Louisiana, Buddy Roemer, right. (*Credit: Rhett Powell.*)

one subject to the other, and I talk to all kinds of interesting people."

While Mayor McGlothin is talking, he is also busily and intricately cutting the hair of someone who sits still and smiles. Mayor McGlothin continues, "Look, I got vaccinated with a phonograph needle when I was a baby, and I have been talking ever since. Of course, it's easy to talk and it's easy to cut hair. The trick is to do them together."

Now he's brushing off his customer, snapping off his bib sheet and helping the customer out of the chair before beckoning to the next one. "While in office," says Mayor McGlothin, "I barber twice a week, and on the weekends, I am a vocalist in a local band called "Easy Eddy and The Party Rockers."

Glen McGlothin sings with the band, Easy Eddie and The Partyrockers.
(*Credit: Rhett Powell.*)

He begins combing the customer's hair prior to cutting it. "When you come back four years from now, I'll either be a good mayor and they'll have my name on that sign coming into town—or everybody will say, 'Well, they hung him on that tree over yonder.' "

Like all good barbers, Glen closely follows trendsetting hair styles of high-profile personalities from athlete Brian Bosworth to anchorman Dan Rather and discourses learnedly on mohawks, flat-tops and the centimeter differences in fashionable lengths.

His last words to me were that he didn't consider himself a politician, "but the longer I am one, the more I sound like one. Barbering is a sound living. I like being mayor. I get a chance to help people. And singing is my outlet."

People in Ferriday are in love with words and like to use lots of them whenever they can. Take, for example, the multiple first names they give their children. To them "Cora" feels too quickly said. "Cora Sue" is much more satisfying. People love to talk, love to say sentences which contain as many words as possible, love to finish sentences with the up-in-the-air question mark, offering a pause for you to join in if so inclined. Surprisingly, I never once came across a monologist in Ferriday. Conversation is a dialogue to which you are invited to reply, and you'd better give your best, because they have been giving theirs. In general, Ferridians tend to avoid lame and generalized verbs like "take" or "make" for the more vigorous ones. A man "hits the lick on his hair" to smooth it, "scoops up a nickle," the book is "pulled out of the shelf" and "the sun pokes out." You "wrap your hand around a Coke," you "wind down the road," a chill "flickers up your back" and you "vibrate with fatigue." When offering an opinion, they "believe" rather than "guess" or "think." It is a mistake to think their speech ungrammatical; they are simply following different rules.

Ferridians easily and enjoyably recall events with a precision of detail that a trial lawyer might despair of wresting out of his star witness. I noticed that the good Ferridian conversationalist often employed "the rule of three," whereby, if you want to drive home a point, you say it three times, each time slightly differently. As a character in Lewis Carroll explains, "What I say three times is true." Thus Clyde Webber, clerk of court, says of Jerry Lee, "His mother could never straighten Jerry Lee out. They lived two doors down and he could do no wrong as far as she was concerned. No matter what he did, it was somebody else's fault." Or a man explaining to me about his wife's leaving him: "No, she won't come back. She didn't like the marriage. She said it was too confining for her, and she wanted to be around more people."

———

I met Austin Wilson in a room off the *Concordia Sentinel*'s offices with his friend R. T. "Bonnie" Bonnette. Bonnie, an old newspaper man, is now a columnist. We are talking about the rolling store owned by Bonnie's dad, his career as a postmaster and his career as a reporter, when suddenly he breaks off to say, "Here's Austin now." I turn to see a powerfully built, silver-haired man who carries the outdoors in with him.

At sixty-eight, Austin Wilson is sleek and well-tended. His eyes seem to glitter. He and Bonnie begin talking back and forth, and I am slowly drawn into the companionship of good conversation that isn't "made" but flows over a variety of topics from farming and Civil War cemeteries to the difference between Huey and Earl Long. ("Huey was straight down the middle," says Austin. "Either you was for him or he ruined you. But Earl would play with you and think he could win you over.") The talk went back to Depression days and Huey's promise of a chicken every Sunday for all. "That was *wealth*. That was high eating," comments Austin, who had been through it.

Listening to these old-timers talking together, a feeling of euphoria gradually steals over me, a feeling of timelessness, weightlessness, punctuated by laughter, a feeling that everything is all right, including things that are not.

It was from Austin that I heard for the first time of the

Austin Wilson.
(Credit: Rhett Powell.)

Mrs. Glen S. Waddell,
Ferriday's favorite teacher
for decades. *(Credit: Russell
Campbell.)*

legendary teacher Mrs. Glen S. Waddell. Perhaps in a small town more than anywhere else, the gifted school teacher stands out (as with Claire Chennault and his stepmother, Lottie) as someone in a position of power able to detect and encourage the potential of her students. Mrs. Waddell was singled out as their favorite teacher by such disparate people as Son Swaggart, pharmacist Russell Campbell, Frances Thomas Smith, Edna Gilley, Mickey's sister, Austin Wilson and Hubert McGlothin, in other words, four decades of schoolchildren. Of all the teachers Austin ever had, "I believe the one that did more for me in my lifetime was Mrs. Glen S. Waddell, our English teacher. She taught you so you'd learn. She gave you guidance. She was raised in Illinois, and her favorite topic was to tell you about the time Jim Thorpe beat the whole University of Illinois football team. Oh, she'd take great delight in telling you about this big university come to Carlisle to eat up this little old Indian school, and instead, Indian Jim Thorpe turned around and licked them."

It is interesting that Mrs. Waddell, the students' choice, was not a sweet, patient, easygoing person but a stern disciplinarian, and her ex-students recount without rancor her high temper and how any boy causing trouble would be grabbed by the hair and slapped soundly in his face. Says Austin, "You better not be caught on school grounds with cigarettes or chewing tobacco. She had a stick to make you study. You had a whole bunch of rules and they was good for your students. I treasure those times with her and remembered them afterward."

By the time Hubert McGlothin was a schoolboy, Mrs. Waddell had mellowed. She was assistant principal and librarian and "everything else." Says Hubert, "She just loved us boys, and she gave us all kinds of attention. If we got into trouble and were sent to the principal's office, we'd just stop inside Miss Waddell's and she'd write us a permit and send us on back."

Mrs. Waddell's fame was not only local, but spread to higher academic circles. Says Austin, "When I went to LSU, they asked me who my English teacher was and when I said

Mrs. Glen S. Waddell, they just hollered, 'Next!' They knew if you passed under her, you didn't have any worries so far as college work."

Austin went to LSU in 1942 on a football scholarship. A movie he saw in November of that year changed his life. "I saw *Sergeant York*. It cost two bits at the Odeon. And that's when I had to jump up and join the army because I was so scared the war was going to get over before I could get there because Sergeant York was killing all the Germans."

In December, Austin enlisted in the army and was sent to England for his paratrooper training (fourteen years after Chennault worked out the new concept of paratroopers and was told by the army brass to "stop that parachute nonsense before someone is hurt"). Paratroopers had become a vital branch of the army.

Mark Twain was not the only American to find being abroad funny. Austin remembers in wartime London that he invaded the Piccadilly Square, as he calls it. Also, "I went dancing at the place in Hammersmith, the biggest dancing hall I believe I've ever seen in my life. They had three bands in there. Never silent. Something going on all the time. And the English people started dancing. We called it 'bicycling,' you know what I mean? The girls would start backing up. The boys would go forward and they'd go round the floor in a circle. If you got out of the circle, you was in trouble. You couldn't get back in it again. And the GIs would be out there in their boots and rubber-soled shoes, and you'd see streaks going all over the floor."

One day, an English officer came into his barracks, said he'd heard Austin liked hunting and invited him along. A fervent sportsman, Austin accepted with alacrity, boasting to the other enlisted men that the English officers liked him so much they were even going to take him bird hunting. In the truck, Austin asked them when they were going to give him a gun. He wasn't going to have a gun, they explained, because he was to be one of the beaters, going out in the field before them and beating the bushes to stir up the birds. Meanwhile, the officers would be sitting and waiting. When he'd raised

the birds, he was to go back to the army vehicle and the
officers would do the hunting. "Next time they asked me to
go with them, I said, 'No sir, I lost my feeling for it.' "

Austin took an active part in the D-Day invasion.

> The first time I flew over Normandy, I had something
> happen to me I will always set back and wonder at. I never
> been that scared in all my life. I was sitting up in that
> plane and we was going into Normandy and I was scared
> to death. And I wasn't by myself, because the men
> sounded like a bunch of motors going on with their knees
> knocking back there. And I can tell you today that my
> daddy talked to me, just as sure as he was sitting beside
> me. He said, "Son, you asked for this. Now you be man
> enough to face it." And I can remember that because it
> eased me off. But I ain't never been that scared in all my
> life. See, I'd let my mouth overload my wagon, and I was
> trying to figure out some way to get out of this, but there
> wasn't any. Boy, they tell you—you won't pray? You call
> them a liar.

When Austin came home, he became an oil contractor,
first in Mexico and then offshore in Louisiana. He was
working for another oil company in Ferriday when he retired
in June of 1984.

After having seen the world, why go back to Ferriday? He
thinks for a minute and then says quietly, "Lord, Lord, Lord.
Well, it's home. I could have followed the oil companies away
from here and made more money overseas than I was making,
but, well, Ferriday is home to me. And all my family was in
this part of country, and I love to hunt and fish, and I miss
very few seasons. We're just an old country family," he
concludes, and you feel him drawing sustenance from this
deep source of comfort.

Austin, as he says, misses few hunting seasons, which
means that a great deal of the winter he is up at 5:00 A.M.
and doesn't return until after dark. This time of year is wild
turkey season. Like many dedicated hunters, he has great
admiration and affection for his prey and a deep rapport with
them. In season, when the turkeys fly over Ferriday, he goes
early to the woods every day and talks to them. He makes hen

gobbling noises to which they respond. "I spend quite a lot of time with them in conversation. They are the hardest bird to shoot. They can see better, hear better than any other birds. And they can run on the ground as fast as a bear."

When Austin retired, he looked forward to peace and contentment for the rest of his life. He felt he had more than attained it when he and his wife, Audie, adopted from birth the child of their daughter. They named her Crystal Renee and they called her their change-of-life child, for indeed, she had wonderfully changed their lives.

On September 28, 1987, Crystal Renee, aged seven, fell off a horse. Her head hit a rock, and twenty-three hours later, she was dead. His other grandchildren, the twins, visit the couple often, and though he takes much joy in them and

Austin Wilson
with his hounds.
(*Credit: Rhett Powell.*)

retains his philosophical balance, his cheerfulness, his love of domestic animals (he has several hound dogs and a coyote called Coty that he has raised from birth), the tragedy of Crystal Renee never leaves him.

———

De Toqueville wrote 150 years ago that "the singular prosperity and growing strength" of the American people "is mainly attributed to the superiority of their women." Now we come to the Steel Magnolias: the group of women in their seventies, eighties and nineties, very much in charge of their lives and of the lives of most other people with whom they come in contact. Steel Magnolia is an apt description. The velvety bloom of the flower is tough, hardy; it seems to last forever (though the description some prefer of these ladies is "the iron fist in the velvet glove").

Perhaps the secret of these women is in how they were raised: they were told they were beautiful, and they were told they were desirable, but they also were told they were capable. They do not feel like victims by the simple expedient of not seeing themselves as victims. They lead lives of perpetual motion, traveling to various parts of the country to visit their children and their children's children, "to help out." And when they return to Ferriday, they are equally active in the community—in their jobs, their churches, the hospital, the town and their gardens. This is true in every walk of life, whether they are plantation managers, insurance brokers or school janitors.

"When it comes to running things," says Mayor McGlothin, "I tell you what: ladies can get it better organized, I believe, because men, we sit around and argue about things. And ladies, they just start doing it. At least, that's been the way it is with everything I do. Like in a men's club and all of that, we always—all the men—we always argue about what ought to be done. The ladies, they just cut right through it and start doing it. When women seem to get ready to do something, hey, they jump on it both feet and go ahead."

———

The Steel Magnolias, left to right, Ira Rogillio, Mae Jones, Blanche
Chauvin and Doris Morris at Doris Morris's home. (*Credit: Rhett
Powell.*)

Blanche Chauvin, nee Alwood, in her nineties, is the
daughter of Charles Alwood, who came to Delhi Plantation
to help Uncle Elmo Porter farm at the turn of the century.

Blanche remembers the little school on Lake St. John she
went to in a horse and buggy before going to Ferriday High.
Over and again, the movies in Ferriday are a matchmaking
ground, and it was at the picture show that Blanche met
Arthur Chauvin. Says Blanche, "After I married, I was a
joiner. I joined everything that came along. I was a member
of the Auxiliary American Legion, a charter member of the
Methodist Church, a member of the Eastern Star, and the
United Methodist Women and the Garden Club." She raised
eight children. What she remembers most vividly of the
Depression days was feeling blessed "because my children
were healthy. We couldn't afford to pay a doctor's bill, much
less get sick."

Her friends still tease her by reminding her how, whenever her children became unmanageable, she simply popped
them all in the car and drove around till they quieted down.

In 1979, Blanche was chosen Louisiana Mother of the

Year. Each town in Louisiana had a Women's Club that solicited recommendations. The minister recommended Blanche as did the superintendent of education and the mayor of Ferriday. She says, "It was one of the highlights of my life and a total surprise. The prize was a week in Hollywood. I loved it."

Blanche's husband, Arthur, was town marshall for twelve years. "It was a trying time in my life. It was busy and bloody. He'd come home bloody. I never had a peaceful moment when he was marshall. Ferriday was a tough town then, sure enough tough."

Frances Thomas Smith, in her seventies, a widow for twenty years, runs the plantation she inherited from her father. I meet her as she comes out of her Ford van. She is gray-haired, in a work shirt, blue-jeaned and sneakered. Inside the van, all is fitted and compartmentalized. In the back, for instance, there is plenty of space for produce, supplies, livestock and a good-size refrigerator. In the front seat, neatly fitted into the dashboard and flanking her, is a coffee mug holder, an ice bucket with ice, fitted glasses, sodas and a tray full of chewing gum and life savers of every imaginable color and flavor. Her CB radio is in constant use. The left door of the cab bears the legend "Get it together." Frances lives in two places, her plantation and her van.

In the middle of her voluble conversation that radiates all over the place, she will suddenly insert some knife-sharp comment like: "We put on country ways because we can get away with more."

Frances has long been a master at playing the farm girl with positive results. At LSU, she soon disarmed the city slickers by having her daddy send his famous Alberta peaches, which were as big as cantaloupes. And he didn't stop there. To smooth her way further, he sent peaches to the LSU football team.

Frances chose a farm topic for her English paper; it was returned with the comment, "I certainly do appreciate you as a student, Frances. I feel like my education has been completed now that I know how to raise pecans."

Her father also cleaned a whole little pig for her home economics class. "So I could stuff it and bake it with an apple in its mouth. I always got points for something like that."

Doris Morris, in her late seventies, remembers that she was happiest as a child and adolescent playing basketball, and that it was her basketball scholarship that got her to college. She still moves with the grace of an athlete. Another thing she remembers is the black taffeta dress trimmed with orange velvet that her mother made for her. Having warts on her feet at the time, she remembers having to go barefoot in the dress, even to church. Miraculously, an itinerant wart-remover came to town, and she woke up one morning bliss-fully wartless. As well as her numerous community activities, it was her idea to dress volunteer hospital workers in pink, so that to this day, they are called Pink Ladies. She worked closely building a community center intended espe-cially for children "but the police jury did not take this into account. After it was built, we used it for a while, and the children began to tear it up, and we had to repair it too much, so we changed it to a library." For years, she ran Ferriday's largest and most successful dress shop. "If you're not trying to improve things, what are you contributing to that community?" she asks.

Ira Rogillio, eightysomething years old, very much the southern belle in manner, is a former school teacher and nine years a widow of the state trooper Gene Rogillio, who rounded up the Hairston Gang without firing one shot (this was the gang that went into Ferriday every night to help build Leona Sumrall's church). Like Blanche, Ira met her husband at the picture show. She says, "He always said he came to Ferriday for deer hunting—and found a dear."

Ira is still romantically attached to her late husband as to a beau ideal. She recalls him with "his beautiful physique— he had such a beautiful physique—I can see him now standing in the doorway right there," she points, "in his best gray suit saying to me, 'How do I look? Hmmm? Hmmm? How do I look?'" And then there falls that stillness that preceeds a surge of emotion, and tears fall unashamedly down her cheeks.

The importance of public tears in Ferriday cannot be overstressed. They are always appropriate, not a source of weakness but a source rather of pride; by shedding them, you are expressing your deepest feelings. Jimmy Swaggart's "I have sinned" sobs must be seen in this context. Public tears, i.e., allowing people to observe your deepest feelings, is very different from allowing them to observe your whining or falling apart. The most popular sheriff Ferriday ever had was Noah Cross. The *Concordia Sentinel* published a picture of him, on taking office for his eighth term, and the caption read, "Sheriff Noah Cross, weeping freely, was sworn in Saturday . . . He held the tears back as the oath was administered, but moments later, cried publicly. Cross faces a Federal prison term."

Grown men fondly look back at their childhoods to find Sheriff Cross always there arranging transport for them to see a ball game they didn't want to miss. Cross's reply to people who jeered at him hauling a group of youngsters who were not old enough to vote off on a trip was, "But I still plan to be sheriff when they are old enough to vote." Unfortunately, his tenure as sheriff took a familiar route—kickbacks, FBI investigation, grand jury indictment, followed by several trials. He served a short term in prison and came back to Ferriday to a triumphant welcome-home parade. Noah Cross sobbed loudly at every funeral he went to, whether he knew the deceased or not. His critics swore that Cross always put an onion in his jacket to speed the process. Mrs. Ben Green well remembers her daughter's wedding because, just as the bride and groom walked up the aisle, loud, uncontrollable sobbing broke out. The daughter, thinking it was her father, experienced a pang of annoyance—her father had *promised* not to! But it wasn't her father, it was Noah Cross.

It was none other than Mrs. Ben Green, now eighty-seven years old, mother of ten children, who way back was selling a ticket to Jimmy Swaggart at the Arcade, when he heard the voice of the Lord telling him not to go in there.

"Jimmy," said Mrs. Green at the time, "do you want to go in? If not, there are others behind you."

But selling tickets on Friday and Saturday was just one thing she did during her busy week. On Sunday, she was receptionist at the Patricia Motel. Mrs. Ben Green, for many years, planned the meals for Ferriday High School's cafeteria. Now she is the most popular caterer around. She is a superior cook. Her shrimp gumbo is superb. Put it in the freezer and you can eat it for days. She knows what the town likes to eat and drink down to a T, not only the main course, but before and after: "Well, of course, they're chocoholics, all of them in Ferriday, so any kind of chocolate pie or cake is fine." And to get things going? "Ferriday is a big Bloody Mary town."

On the polished surfaces of her tables are china figurines and bowls of fragrant roses from her garden. Organdy curtains stir in the breeze. Mrs. Green took up catering because she needed the money. "We had bread, you know," she says, "but this was for jam. I wanted jam."

Jeffrey Gremillion. (*Credit: Jeffrey Gremillion private collection, 1990.*)

Nineteen-year-old Jeffrey Gremillion of Ferriday, now in his third year at Central University at Lafayette, wants it all: bread and jam and caviar and champagne. This year, he was elected President of the College of Arts and Humanities and Behaviorial Sciences. He is the film critic for the college newspaper and one of the editors of its yearbook. He is active in the drama club and sometimes gets a part in a college play. Back in his senior year of high school, he won first prize for journalism in a statewide contest. He wants to be an actor— or a writer—or a lawyer—or a politician. So many interests; so many possible careers. His mother is beautiful, and his father, good-looking and one of the youngest judges ever to sit on the bench.

"I'm tired of everybody saying, 'Oh, you're from Ferriday, aren't you? That's where Jerry Lee Lewis is from.' " He says, "Someday, they're going to say that's where Jeffrey Gremillion is from."

13

MRS. U. B. EVANS AND PETE GREGORY

I have saved her until the last, although she was the first person I looked up when I originally came to Ferriday. She is Mrs. U. B. Evans, aged ninety-five, and she is the most respected person in Ferriday today. A founding member of a powerful group of women known as Friends of Ferriday, for the last forty years, she has been Ferriday's truest friend, actively involved in every aspect of the town. She is omnipresent. She rules her domain by telephone. Should you ask Ferriday's Chamber of Commerce for further information, the number they give you is that of—who else?—Mrs. Evans.

Recently, regretfully, she turned down the honor of leading Ferriday's Christmas parade as grand marshal because of the inclemency of the weather.

Honors have been showered upon Mrs. U. B. Evans. A renowned horticulturist and archeologist, she is a byword in these circles throughout the world. She has a species of lily, the Amaryllis Evansae, named after her, and an Indian arrowpoint, Evans Point, resides in New York's Museum of Natural History. In 1978, she was the first person in Loui-

217

siana to receive its Distinguished Service to Agriculture award.

Her birthplace was a small town in Kentucky. "I was born into a horticultural world. I loved it always," she explains. "My father taught me wildflowers, and my mother taught me the other flowers from our own garden. Archeology I taught myself." When she was quite young, she moved with her family to Alexandria, Louisiana, where she graduated from high school at the young age of fourteen. This accomplishment she shrugs off with, "I don't know, maybe it was an accident." She spent a year in business college and then went to work in the office of the man she later married, Mr. U. B. "Bob" Evans, an electrical engineer, sugar chemist and history buff.

From the time of their marriage until Mr. Bob's death in 1968, they were apart only once, and then for less than two weeks. It was a rare dovetailing of interests that these two formidably intelligent people enjoyed in their marriage, and one subject above all consumed them utterly: Louisiana—its history, its prehistory, its plants, birds, animals and people— to which purpose they traveled over every inch of its countryside, or as she puts it, "I think we knew every pigtrack."

Traveling around in the 1920's, they found themselves more and more searching for that special, that ideal, that utopian place where they would settle down, more and more realizing that it was not New Orleans or Baton Rouge calling them, but a plantation "right up in the country."

In the early 1930's, they acquired that plantation. It dates back to 1834 and is called Haphazard, deriving its name from the fact that, in order to get from the front to the back of the place, you have to zigzag around a number of lakes. It is located in Frogmore, a small community just outside Ferriday. It is at present a working plantation. Four other farmers work it, as well. How these 12,000 acres of fertile land came to be up for sale was the direct result of a disaster. In 1927, the Mississippi River overflowed into the worst flood in the history of the United States, causing the devastation of 1,300,000 acres of land and making 300,000 people homeless. Haphazard's former owners, feeling the odds too high against them, just walked off and turned it over to a bank in New Orleans, who subsequently sold it to the Evanses. For the next few years, they went back and forth repairing the plantation until around 1940, in what was to be an auspicious advent for both them and Ferriday, they were able to settle permanently into their spiritual and physical home. It is here that Mrs. Evans began to cultivate her garden in earnest.

———

Mrs. Evans, as befits her Renaissance character, loves politics with all its thrust and parry and is herself a skilled and effective Louisiana politician with a lifetime of friends in high places. Urged to reminisce on this aspect of her many-faceted personality, she obliges:

> Well, I think this is a right nice story. Earl Long was governor, and he was a very good friend of mine and he told me in 1949 there was no department of horticulture in any of the colleges. And he told me that if I got a bill introduced and put it through the House, he would sign it and get money for it. I was serving as state president of the Garden Club at the time, and I accepted the challenge. At two o'clock one morning, I got word from the governor that if I didn't get to his office by seven o'clock that morning [a three-and-a-half-hour drive to Baton Rouge], there wouldn't be any money. And I was there. What had happened, see, was that two colleges had gotten into a fight over who was going to have a horticultural department, so the governor and I sat down with them and we really smoothed things over, and the result was that both schools, LSU and Southwestern in Lafayette, got outstanding departments of horticulture.

What Mrs. Evans leaves unsaid is how she, a true communicator, was able to stimulate Governor Long's interest in *her* interest in the first place to the extent that he was prepared to do something about it.

———

A lecturer all her life, notably in LSU's classrooms for a quarter of a century, Mrs. Evans has written many learned articles. For many years, she also wrote a column, "Garden Gossip," for the statewide electric co-operative's monthly paper, which was followed breathlessly by some 125,000 readers. In one column, when she mentioned she would send marigold seeds on request, the magazine was so flooded with requests, it had to stop operations to fill the orders. These informative columns have recently been collected and published by the Natchez Pilgrimage Garden Club.

From her ninetieth year on, she has been writing what she calls "my little books" under her own name of Jo N. Evans. So far, four of them have been published, three beautifully illustrated and calligraphed by nature artist Lisa Brunelli: *Travelers in the Moonlight and Other Louisiana stories, Wings in the Night* (now in its second edition) *Four Seasons of a Southern Gardner,* co-authored with her granddaughter, Joan Pitcher, and published November, 1990, and a booklet called *My Mother's Garden.* They are packed with her vast and precise knowledge of flora and fauna living and growing in her gardens, lakes and bayous. She also deals with things long gone in the Catahoula Indian history of a neighboring parish. These books she dedicates, "To all young children and grown-up children who love the outdoors." She is too modest. I challenge the most fanatic cliff-dwelling city lover who actively loathes the outdoors, who is terminally bored by nature, to open any of these and not quickly sink spellbound into it. Her prose, in its stark condensation and lucidity, most closely resembles the poetry of the Japanese haiku. Here is her description of a Louisiana bird, the anhinga:

> The courtship of the anhinga is as beautiful as a ballet. This is surprising, as he is an ugly bird until he performs his dance on the water. This water bird is called the "water turkey" by local residents. If the anhinga is shot, he swims underwater and pulls it out and heals himself.

The reader is always aware of the eternal watcher, quiescent, sentient in familiar surroundings—a porch, a lake, or perhaps a bedroom—suddenly struck by an epiphany.

"One summer afternoon, we were sitting on our front porch. A quail was walking around the yard calling, 'bob-white!' A sly mocking bird in the cypress tree would answer, 'bob-white!' The quail again called 'bob-white,' and the mocker replied, 'bob-white!' The third time as the mocking bird said 'bob-white,' the quail knew she was being fooled by an impostor. A real male quail would have replied, 'Are-the-peas alRIGHT?' "

High in the sky, writes Mrs. Evans, a wounded duck is being pitched back and forth between two eagles. This is sometimes an aerial game, sometimes a courtship ritual.

Perhaps most moving of her stories is her few lines about the ruby-crowned kinglet:

There is a fan-shaped window in my bedroom. My husband, ill for two years, remained in the bed at all times. He did much reading, and we took care of him. A ruby-crowned kinglet spent those two winters in the window. The bird would peek through the window and watch my husband. Going into the third winter of illness, my husband died in October. We watched and watched for the cute bird that winter, but it never returned.

━━━━━

I remember, on my first visit to Haphazard to meet this extraordinary woman, how odd it felt to be driving through a vast dreamscape so flat. It was disorienting to be gazing at it all from eye level instead of viewing the panorama from above or below. Countrysides are hilly, and when a horizon hits a hill, the vista ends abruptly, but these free reaches go on to infinity. We drive through sunlit hills and pastures punctured with mysterious, dark shadowed lakes and bayous surrounded by huge ancient cypresses and oaks that grow both on the banks and in the water. Their dense leaves are

Cotton fields, pecan groves and, now and then, an oil well.
(*Credit: Rhett Powell.*)

shaded black underneath, while on top, they sparkle the color of bright green licorice in the sun.

A sort of miasma of ignorance rises inside me, a psychic numbness increased by not being able to give things their proper names. Are those pelicans? Or cranes? Or what? And what sort of crops are beginning to grow in those fields? The small green shafts peeking aboveground give me no clue. And why are the lone clusters of trees sticking up like that in the middle of the fields? (I am told by my companion that they were planted there for the purpose of giving shade to the workers during lunchtime).

In the haystack of my mind, pieces of jumbled agenda stick into it like needles: all the things I want to say to Mrs. Evans, all the things I want to ask her, all the things I want her help with. I really want a lot from her.

At last, we drive through one gate, then another, and finally, we are at Haphazard. True to its name, the house itself has a haphazard, much lived-in look. There seem to be several entrances that could serve equally as front or back doors. Behind which door will I find Mrs. Evans? I know she shares the house with her great-grandaughter, her husband and her little great-great-grandson, Jeffrey. I choose the right one.

Mrs. Evans receives me in her bedroom, now her main living quarters. On the walls hang paintings by young relatives, and in the background is a cherrywood bed, handmade specially for her and her husband many, many years ago and crafted so that it required no nails. It went under in the flood of 1945 for three days, but its wood had been so carefully tempered that it survived intact. She is sitting in an easy chair by her radio and telephone. Her features are pronounced; her white hair is curly; her dress is blue with a red belt. She wears her gaunt, thin longevity like a mist.

Mrs. Evans is blind and has been for the past few years.

Her voice is Southern sharp, filled with enthusiasm. Her first words are about country matters. "I want to tell y'all, you would have had a seven-ring circus here last night. Sugar, our shy little mare, raised on a bottle, foaled, and my family came running in here at 10:30 in the evening. Sugar's baby!

Mrs. Jo N. Evans displays her childhood dolls. *(Credit: Jarrett Reeves, 1990.)*

Sugar's baby! Sugar's baby! Little two-and-a-half-year-old Jeffrey was so excited, he told me how his daddy lifted up the colt and put him on dry straw and so on, and they all had to telephone till nearly one in the morning telling everyone that Sugar had a baby."

It was a natural progression in Mrs. Evans's character, while cultivating her own garden, to cultivate the gardens of her Ferriday world. For years, she has planted bulbs in all the gardens of her Ferriday friends and the town itself. Her husband had a fondness for Bradford ornamental pear trees. At his death, she planted many of them in his memory. Since then, with the help and cooperation of the Friends of Ferriday, she has overseen the planting of about 1,000 of these trees in Concordia Parish. There are about 600 of them in Ferriday. Viewed from an airplane, they look, when they are in bloom, like whitecaps on an ocean.

Friends of Ferriday has been in action for forty-six years. "It started in the flood of nineteen-hundred-and-forty-five . . ." says Mrs. Evans. One spring night, she and her husband sat on their front porch listening to the waters rolling through their woods. The Mississippi had again

Some Bradford ornamental pears Mrs. Evans had planted near
Ferriday's medical center. (*Credit: Rhett Powell.*)

flooded. Its waters covered the entire plantation and came
midway up the house. In contrast to the behavior of the
previous owners, the Evanses did not just walk off and turn
it over to the bank. They stayed and were kept busy shooting
the snakes that rose with the water, in order to save the birds
from them. They also plugged every small hole in every wall
of the house to keep the snakes from entering it. When the
flood subsided, Mrs. Evans and fifteen other women, "all
leaders," announced themselves to be Friends of Ferriday and
told the mayor they planned "to bring the town back out of
the mire." Being no fool, he gave them his total support.

Allowing for the men getting drunk on Saturday night
and recovering on Sunday, these Steel Magnolias rolled up
their sleeves and waded into town early Monday morning,
flourishing brooms, brushes, mops, pails and rubber boots.
Cattle were roaming all over town. Sewage was running in
the street. Everything was dirty and smelly. They comman-
deered a big hay mower to clean the streets, driving it
themselves back and forth through the town. Naturally, their
activities spurred on the rest of the good citizens; but to the
uninspired was added a special Evans prod: "The way we got

them to help us is we all took our Kodaks with us. And if they didn't help clean, why we'd take a picture of them. Pretty soon, everybody was working."

Recently, Friends of Ferriday have been busy laying out a pretty park where once there was a thriving depot which fell into disuse. Editorials in the local paper always invoke Mrs. Evans's name when pleading with people to pick up their litter and help beautify the parish.

Mrs. Evans has publishing plans for the future. One book will be called *Dog Tales and Other Stories.* "My husband and I loved bird dogs, and we raised and trained them." She is also working on a book called *Plantation Bells.* "They were wonderful, useful things that could be heard for miles and often of great beauty as well. If a plantation bell rang a certain number of times, people knew exactly what it was telling them. It could be summoning them to eat or to rest. It could signal arrivals and departures. It was very useful in disasters like fire or a death in the family. They rang for the plantation workers to come to work. They rang for them to come to dinner. There was a mule whose name was 'Dinner-bell.' It didn't matter what she was doing, when the dinner bell rang she came in to get her dinner."

Mrs. Evans has a wide experience of a great many things and a wonderful way of communicating them. Like a heartening number of elderly people in Ferriday—with "a bit of age on them," as they say there, and a bit of experience— she has sifted the wheat from the chaff in her reminiscences. Obscuring underbrush and brambles have been cleared away, and now the essence of her stories unfolds in all its clarity. For everyone she encounters, she harvests her knowledge, simplifies it and gives it as wisdom. The feeling of security that the very intelligent inspire in us has not begun to be explored. There is a sign on entering Ferriday with the names of well-known people connected with it. Mrs. U. B. Evans's name is in the center and written larger than the rest.

Whenever Jerry Lee Lewis and, more recently, his cousin Jimmy Swaggart land in the soup, and news of their scandals reverberates around the world, inquiring reporters from all over head straight for their hometown. This can be tiresome to its natives.

For Mrs. Evans, the more rampageous of these newsmen are sometimes a sore trial. One arrived with a bottle of whiskey, freely availing himself of it throughout the interview and behaving quite crudely. Asked what she thought of Ferriday's black mayor, Sammy Davis, Jr., she gave what some would consider a color-blind answer. She said she would have no objection to a black mayor who could do things, but that she felt things went under during his term as mayor. "He wouldn't work with us [Friends of Ferriday]. We tried. He didn't want that. It's too bad. He had the opportunity to make something." She added she'd always lived around colored people and that there were no better friends on earth. At the end, the reporter asked her why, though she's in her nineties, her mind works as well as it does. She replied "Because I don't drink and I don't smoke." He was doing both. When the article came out, she was portrayed as your usual Southern bigot.

I wonder for a bad moment if, after experiences like this, I dare ask her for other people who might further my quest.

At this point, the mail arrives. She asks me to open it and read it to her. The first letter is from a friend she used to go hunting wildflowers with. The second is from a woman planning to write a book on Louisiana pre-history as well as "the personalities involved." She is looking for insights and anecdotes and recollections of these personalities. I read out the names that follow, and Mrs. Evans explains them as I go.

"James Ford?"

"Museum of Natural History," she says.

"Winslow Walker?"

"He did the big mounds at Jonesville."

"Frank Setlzer?"

"Smithsonian also."

"Caroline Dormon?"

"A wonderful nature artist and writer, published a lot of books."

"Ed Neild?"

"An architect who put up a lot of money to do things with."

"Pete Gregory?"

"I raised Pete Gregory. That's Dr. Gregory, Professor of Anthropology at Northwestern University, Natchitoches."

My instinct stirred. Or is instinct just reasoning speeded up? I rushed in: "That's who I want to meet." I find I am holding my breath for her answer.

"Well, you're in luck. He's on an archeological dig in Marksville, which is not far from here. Operator?" says Mrs. Evans into the phone, "I'd like to get you to dial this number. No, I don't see to dial. No, that's all, all right honey. Pete? I have a friend here. I think you're going to spend a good while with her . . ."

———

The next day, I arrive at Marksville somewhat surprised that my quest has brought me to an archeological site. I allow myself some disciplined excitement. It is an important site of three ancient Indian civilizations who occupied it from 1500 B.C. to A.D. 500. It is a site of incredible richness because it has not been disturbed since these three Indian occupations, and it is still held sacred by the most recent Tunica Indians, who dwell nearby.

Pete Gregory, a friendly man in his mid-fifties, clear-eyed and full of laughter, turns out to be the direct link between Jimmy, Jerry Lee, Mickey and Mrs. U. B. Evans.

While Jerry Lee was obsessed with mischief and music, and Jimmy Swaggart was running away from God, and Mickey was in love with Geraldine, young Hiram "Pete" Gregory, their contemporary and neighbor, when not playing with them, was prowling around Concordia Parish, looking for broken pottery. When he was even younger, his grandmother had given him an Indian point she had found when they were sharecropping. "When she gave it to me, she told me the Indians had made it, and I got very interested and all through high school, I prowled around Concordia, Tensas and Catahoula Parishes looking for sites and digging.

"One day, when I was about fourteen, I was out in a plowed field picking out broken pottery and a lady stopped and asked me what I was doing. I said, 'Just picking up this old Indian stuff,' and she said, 'You want to come into the house. We've got some of that.' And I said, 'Sure,' and that was how I met Mrs. U. B. Evans and her husband Mr. Bob, and they had a really nice collection and a really nice library. We had a pretty good library in Ferriday, and I worked as a janitor there when I was in high school. I would go sweep up and use these books. One day, Mrs. Evans said to me, 'What do you want to do?' and I said, 'Well, I kind of think I'd like to be an archeologist,' and she just laughed at hearing somebody she'd met out in the cotton field even knowing the word. Eventually, the Evanses made their library available to me. I used to stay there for hours, and Mrs. Evans eventually let me take the books home and bring them back.

"Haphazard was never glorious but it was very interesting. It takes you pretty much through the history of the parish, what with the windows in the back bedroom coming out of the old parish antebellum courthouse, and the cast iron steps are all steps from another old building, and some of the brick in the house came from an antebellum cotton gin." It was, above all, the house of two scholars. There was no card playing at Haphazard, no games, no dancing. Mrs. Evans and Mr. Bob read far into the night lying in their bed of cherrywood, fooling the rooster, who crowed at their lamplight, into thinking it was daytime. Says Pete, "The Evanses were always working, in the sense that there were always people in and out of the place and from all over that had to be collaborated with—doctors, horticulturists, archeologists."

Continually they supported the young people they believed in, paying them to do research for various historians. What it really came down to was that Mr. and Mrs. Evans practically "sugar daddied" most of the young archeologists in the state at that time, and a lot of them, like James Ford and Pete Gregory, went on to become famous.

Mrs. U. B. Evans masterminded young Pete's career every step of the way. When the time was right, she took him to LSU and introduced him to Professor Fred Kniffen, who was head of the anthropology department there. "I remember during this time I used to tell Mrs. Evans, 'You and Dr. Kniffen are doing a sort of high-low on me, good guy, bad guy.' Kniffen being the bad guy. Anyway it got me to LSU, and Dr. Kniffen and I just wrote a book together last year on the Louisiana Indians."

Viewed anthropoligically, what did Pete Gregory make of Ferriday?

"Ferriday is a very complicated place culturally. There are Italians and some Greek families, some Russian and French Jewish families, some German and Irish families. And during my time, there were some Mexican families there, are still some Mexican families there. And Chinese.

"With the Chinese I became great friends. They all went on to be mechanical engineers with all those computers. And here I am an archeologist, so I'm still doing stoop work."

According to Pete, Ferriday was a pretty egalitarian kind of place. After getting his master's degree from LSU, he caught a bus and came home. He got off the bus with his degree under his arm and stopped on the corner near Mr. Nelson's grocery store. They were unloading potatoes. Pete had worked for Nelson as a kid. When Nelson saw him he said, "Did you get your degree?" And Pete said yes. " 'Well, go in there,' said Nelson, 'put it on the damn counter and help me unload these potatoes.' It's that kind of a place," says Pete.

I mentioned that in the short time I had been in Ferriday, I had noticed with what respect elderly people are treated. "It's a southern thing," says Pete. "It all ties in with the oral tradition in the South. Maybe that has to do with the fact that some of them didn't go to school. Jerry Lee's dad, Elmo Lewis, was a wonderful story teller. It goes back to days when people had no television or radio, there was this idea that old people became a repository well. And because of that, these old people are sacred. They are the only place the

Joe-Jim Lee, second-generation Chinese American, and his family, live on Lake St. John. (*Credit: Rhett Powell.*)

young ones can go to find out *what happened*. So they take care of them and listen to them. They were great porch sitters, great talkers, great spinners of tales, and the kids listened a lot. Family musical traditions grew out of the fact that you had to entertain yourself."

It is time for Pete to go back to work. "You sound as though you had a good time growing up," I say.

"Sure, it was a good time. It was a good place to grow up. Well, maybe it wasn't a good place to grow up, but it was interesting—it never got dull growing up there. And there were a lot of good people there. I drifted around widely in that town, so I knew black people, Chinese people, Mexican people. I learned to speak Spanish from Mexican kids there. I did a lot of things I probably couldn't have done somewhere else growing up that, you know, were fun. And if I got bored on one side of town, I could go over to the other side of town."

As he speaks, I seem to see him a young boy, roaming the streets of Ferriday, savoring its cosmopolitan atmosphere at twilight until his mother finds him and calls him in.

And, perhaps the next day or the day after that, Pete, wandering into her cotton field looking for shards, will meet Mrs. Evans for the first time, and they will exchange words that will change his life. It will be a meeting as fortuitous and as miraculous as any of those at the Assembly of God Church.

———

I once asked a Greek what he thought about the Parthenon. "I don't like it or dislike it." he said. "It's just mine."

Frankie says the same thing, though more rapturously. "Ferriday is comforting. Does that make sense, it's comforting? It's a comfort. This is just my heritage. Oh God, I tear up when I think of it. It's something that I would never give up. I could no more sell my home, because I was raised here and this is me. The ground, the house, the atmosphere. I thought when I was young, I've got to leave, and I left. I thought it was the town's fault but it wasn't. I always came home. There's always something to talk about, and there's always something to do. It's just a small little place, but you can get in the car and you can visit and talk and there's not enough time to visit and talk. It would take you twenty years to do all the things in this town if you were raised here. There's no jobs hardly. I realize it, and I forgive everyone that's moved. Don't misunderstand. I realize they have to do this. But as long as they have Ferriday in their hearts and can take it with them, it's all right. I was brought up in this house, and every funeral has been here. Every wake, every wedding that I've been to has been in this house. And receptions and things. I couldn't imagine leaving this place. I'm glued to this town. I know this is just in my mind. I'm in touch and have been able to pick up on it. I can't help it.

Member of Ferriday
High School Band . . .
The band plays on.
(*Credit: Rhett Powell, 1990.*)

Yeah, I mean it's too much to say you're glued to this place, but I am. I'm just glued."

Austin Wilson provides what may be the town's credo: "We was raised an independent people," he says. "We didn't have to follow any leadership. If you had the anxiety or the desire to do anything, well, it was up to you to do it. Nobody seemed to block your way."

Selected Bibliography

Wall, Bennett H., editor. Contributors Charles Edward O'Neil, Joe Gray Taylor, William Ivy Hair, Mark T. Carleton, Michael L. Kurtz. *Louisiana*. The Form Press, 1984.

Taylor, Joe Gray. *Louisiana History*. Norton, 1976.

James, Clayton. *Antebellum Natchez*. Louisiana State University Press, 1968.

Kane, Harnett T. *Natchez on the Mississippi*. William Morrow and Company, 1947.

Holmes, Jack D. L. *Gayoso—The Life of the Spanish Governor in the Mississippi Valley, 1789–1799*. Louisiana State University Press, 1965.

Calhoun, Robert Dabney. *A History of Concordia Parish*. The Louisiana Historical Quarterly, January 1932.

Hanson, Henry, editor. *Louisiana, A Guide to the State*. New revised edition. Hastings House Publishers. New York, 1971.

Chennault, Anna. *Chennault and the Flying Tigers*. Paul S. Ericson, Inc., 1963.

Chennault, Claire Lee. *The Way of a Fighter: Memoires of Claire Lee Chennault*. Editor, Robert Hotz. Putnam, 1949.

Scott, Robert Lee. *Flying Tigers: Chennault of China*. Doubleday, 1959.

Tuchman, Barbara. *Stilwell and the American Experience in China, 1911–1945*. Macmillan, 1971.

Palsson, Leonard and Mary Dale, editors. *Jews in the South*. Louisiana State University Press, 1973.

Fitzgerald, Frances. *Cities on a Hill*. Simon & Schuster, 1987.

Claypool, Bob. *Gilley's*. Delilah/Grove Press, 1980.

Louisiana Folk Life, Vol. 7, Number 2. October 1982.

Guralnick, Peter. *Lost Highway*. Random House, 1979.

Guralnick, Peter. *Feel Like Going Home: Portrait in Blues and Rock 'n Roll*, Vintage Books, 1981.

Tosches, Nick. *Hellfire*. Delacorte Press, 1982.

Lewis, Myra, and Silver, Murray. *Great Balls of Fire*. Virgin Books, London, 1982.

235

Kniffen, Fred; Gregory, Hiram F.; Stokes, George A. *The Historic Indian Tribes of Louisiana*. Louisiana State University Press, Baton Rouge and London, 1987.

Swaggart, Jimmy (with Lamb, Robert Paul). *To Cross a River*. Jimmy Swaggart Ministries. Baton Rouge, Louisiana, 1984.

Murphy, Leona Sumrall. *A Teenager Who Dared to Obey God*. Le Sea Publishing Company, 1985.

Sumrall, Lester (with Conn, J. Stephen). *Miracles Don't Just Happen*. Le Sea Publishing Company. South Bend, Indiana, 1979.

Sumrall, Lester (with Conn, J. Stephen). *Run with the Vision*. Le Sea Publishing Company. South Bend, Indiana, 1986.

Relevant articles in *New York Times, Los Angeles Times, Rolling Stone, Time* magazine, and *People*.

The *Concordia Sentinel:* Centennial issue. Also articles 1988–1991. Ferriday, Louisiana. Publisher, Sam Hanna.

Additional archival material on Howard K. Smith, General Claire Lee Chennault, Jimmy Swaggart and Jerry Lee Lewis supplied by researcher Judy Rehak.

Index

237